D1541891

# Humanistic Perspectives in a Technological World

Georgia Tech | School of Literature, Media and Communication

Ivan Allen College of Liberal Arts

# Humanistic Perspectives in a Technological World

*Humanistic Perspectives in a Technological World*
First Edition
ISBN number: 978-0-9909961-0-1

©2014 School of Literature, Media, and Communication
Ivan Allen College of Liberal Arts
Georgia Institute of Technology

Richard Utz, Editor
Valerie B. Johnson & Travis Denton, Assistant Editors

Layout & Design by Travis Denton

Front & Back Cover and Title Page Images by
Lawrence Yang
www.suckatlife.com

Printed & bound in the United States

School of Literature, Media, and Communication
Georgia Institute of Technology
686 Cherry St.
Atlanta, Georgia 30332-0165
www.lmc.gatech.edu

## Acknowledgements

This volume, a veritable narrative tour through the School of Literature, Media, and Communication (LMC), is first and foremost a communal effort by all the faculty who decided to contribute essays on how they provide humanistic perspectives in a technological world in their research, teaching, and service activities. I am grateful for their giving freely of their valuable time to write these essays. I would also like to acknowledge the support from Ivan Allen College of Liberal Arts Dean, Dr. Jacqueline Jones Royster, who recognized the value added to our School and the College by this project.

Throughout the book you will find statements from numerous faculty, staff, and administrators from all across Georgia Tech about the role our School plays in the larger context of our entire institution. I am grateful to them for adding their "external" perspective to our volume.

Most importantly, I would like to acknowledge my two assistant editors, Dr. Valerie Johnson, a wonderful member of our cohort of c. 40 postdoctoral fellows in LMC, who helped me edit the texts into publishable shape, and Travis Denton, Associate Director of Poetry@Tech, who applied his amazing editorial and design skills to creating the final "look" of our volume. Travis is also responsible for our finding a suitable publisher capable of realizing our specific ideas about the format and quality of paper, color, and cover.

Finally, I would like to thank all who contributed photographs, design advice, and other helpful hints throughout the process.

I hope everyone who receives this book will enjoy reading and sharing it with those who are looking for excitingly interdisciplinary humanities programs at one of the country's premier technological universities.

Richard Utz, Editor

# Humanistic Perspectives
# in a Technological World

"Our world is a fast-paced technologically and scientifically rich environment. At the same time, it is also a place of provocative contrasts and remarkable incongruities among individuals and communities around the globe. The amazing range of work of the School of Literature, Media, and Communication (LMC) helps all of us to understand these complexities from a human-centered perspective, demonstrating in compelling ways that in the Ivan Allen College our work really is innovative at the crossroads of humanities, social sciences, and technology. The LMC group brings to the fore expertise in literary and cultural studies; studies of science, technology, and medicine; performance and communications studies; digital media studies; and more. They are engaging actively in defining problems and addressing challenges with a more holistic view and in developing workable solutions capable of positive sustainable change in our collective efforts in the academic community to make the world a better place. Not only do their analytical and interpretive frameworks add value as we face some of the thorniest issues and challenges the world has ever seen, they create and use innovative tools that help to leverage problem-solving success. They are indeed making a meaningful difference in the knowledge-generating enterprise, in the application of that knowledge to local and global challenges, and in the quality of our lives and experiences."

Jacqueline Jones Royster,
GT Ivan Allen Jr. Chair in Liberal Arts
and Technology and Dean

**"The role that LMC plays in the humanistic side of what our students take away from their Tech experience is more important than ever."**

*Steven W. McLaughlin,*
*Steve W. Chaddick School Chair*
*& Professor, GT School of Electrical*
*and Computer Engineering*

# Richard Utz, Chair
## Literature, Media, and Communication

# Come Join us in the Cloud

The School of Literature, Media, and Communication (LMC) is quite unlike most traditional teaching units in the liberal arts and humanities. Most importantly, it is not organized according to the regular confines of academic disciplines that have dominated how groups of scholars and teachers define and congregate since the late nineteenth century. Thus, while "English" was among the six foundational departments when Georgia Tech was founded in 1888, faculty in our English Department recognized the signs of the times in the early 1990s and reoriented and renamed the unit to critically accompany and even shape the quickly evolving future of academic education. The result of this reorientation, and the realization that complex social questions cannot be solved by any one academic discipline in isolation, is a School that features faculty with specializations in Biomedicine, Communication, Composition, Creative Writing, Critical Race Studies, Cultural Studies, Digital Media, Digital Humanities, Film, Literature, Law, Performance Studies, Science Fiction, Video, and many more. All that still suggests the "English" beginnings of our unit are the curricular offerings of "ENGL 1101" and "ENGL 1102," a course sequence which satisfies the Georgia Board of Regents requirement for composition. However, even these courses, just like LMC's organizational and curricular make-up, bear only a faint resemblance to conventional academic introductions to writing and communication. They offer elements of the kinds of Written, Oral, Visual, Electronic, and Nonverbal (WOVEN) communication with which students are expected to be conversant now and in the future.

Similarly, our two undergraduate majors, both Bachelor of Science degrees, are deeply interdisciplinary and encourage students to be "critical makers" interested in both evaluating AND producing the media (texts, images, games, video, objects, etc.) with which they engage. Our Literature, Media, and Communication (LMC) major allows students to focus on one of six threads from an exciting interdisciplinary banquet of courses: Communication; Literature; Media; Social Justice Studies; Interaction Design; and Science, Technology, and Culture. Our Computational Media (CM) major, which we offer in collaboration with the College of Computing, allows students to select one thread from LMC and one from Computer Science to forge a similarly interconnected experience. CM students may concentrate on Intelligence and Film, Performance, and Media, People and Game Studies, Media and Interaction Design and Experimental Media, to name only a few. Finally, at the graduate level, we provide nationally renowned M.S. and Ph.D. programs in Digital Media which comprise the areas of Arts & Entertainment, Civic Media, and Creativity & Knowledge.

From a distance, of course, LMC resembles somewhat the description you will see if you search for our School acronym on Wikipedia. There, you will find that LMC stands for a nearby "irregular type galaxy," the "Large Magellanic Cloud," a "faint 'cloud' in the night sky of the southern hemisphere," "undergoing vigorous star formation activity." We are indeed "irregular" in that we consciously and joyfully (re)combine and (re)connect what academic specialism has separated over the last 150 years so that our work may have an impact inside and outside the ivory tower. Our "vigorous star formation" includes faculty who garner major grants with the National Science Foundation, the National Endowment for the Humanities, and the Bill and Melinda Gates Foundation, and who disseminate their research in renowned academic publications as well as discuss it publicly on the Colbert Report and MSNBC's Melissa Harris Perry show, in *The Atlantic*, the *Chronicle of Higher Education*, *Inside Higher Ed*, and *Slate.com*. And did I mention that LMC faculty, in addition to national and international recognition, are recent recipients of the Georgia Board of Regents Teaching Excellence Award, the Governor's Award in the Arts and Humanities, and the Georgia Writers Association's Author of the Year Award?

And where have our "star" graduates gone in recent years? At the undergraduate level, their innovative and wide ranging educational experience lands them positions with the Woodruff Arts Center, Turner Classic Movies, the College of William and Mary, Make-A-Wish Georgia, CareerBuilder.com, Graphic Dimensions, Asset Marketing, Huron Consulting, Salesfusion, Electronic Arts, Microsoft, Boeing, AT&T, IBM, General Motors, Google, ThoughtWorks, and Sapient Nitro; at the graduate level, they move on to positions at the University of Georgia, Rensselaer Polytechnic, New York University, or are hired by Nokia, Walt Disney Imagineering, Google, and Turner Broadcasting.

Because our numerous achievements are not always visible in a traditional academic culture still based on segregated disciplines, we thought we should make more transparent what is happening in our fascinating "irregular galaxy." Each of the stories in this volume grants insight into what awaits you, should you choose to join us as student, faculty, staff, or visitor. However, while each of the stories can offer only one "slice" of LMC's activities, reading the entire volume reveals the mission that unites us in spite (or perhaps because) of the diverse nature of our backgrounds, experiences, and specializations: We strive to provide interdisciplinary humanistic perspectives in an increasingly technological world.

Please get in touch if you wish to learn more about how we work at the intersection between science/technology and the humanities/social sciences. Come join us in our very own "cloud."

Richard Utz
Chair & Professor

**"Contributing to, and succeeding in, the 21st century workplace demands using both halves of one's brain, and Georgia Tech's LMC students and graduates are uniquely capable of this. LMC's multi-disciplinary and innovative approach to the humanities in a digital age creates students with marketable skills and bases of knowledge, whether a career in business, industry, or academia is the target."**

*L. Michelle Tullier, PhD,*
*Executive Director, GT Center*
*for Career Discovery and Development*

## Lauren Klein

# Digital Humanities as Method and Mission

My engagement with the digital is the result of an enduring interest in the intersection between technology and education; it has shaped who I was as a student and who I am as a scholar. You might say that I was an early adopter: when I was a child, my family acquired one of the first Apple Macintosh computers, and I spent my afternoons riveted to its black-and-white screen. That experience opened my mind to the possibilities of thinking through technology. In my senior year of high school, I was charged with choosing the yearbook theme. I selected "The Internet," an idea spurred by the launch of the not-yet-ubiquitous Netscape Navigator 1.0. Even then, I was excited by the internet's potential to communicate ideas and information. In college, I discovered Usenet, an early internet discussion system, and began to learn from and collaborate with others online. I created my first website and took my first programming course, and upon graduation, at the tail end of the first dot-com boom, I took my first fulltime job as a web developer.

After several years in the industry—and then an additional year as a bike messenger—I returned to graduate school. By re-entering academia, I hoped to more fully understand the digital culture that surrounded me by exploring the cultural contexts and media forms that gave rise to it. In my research and in my teaching, I continue to seek out connections between past and present, between the scientific and technological concepts that animated earlier centuries, and those that underpin digital life today. It is among my most strongly held scholarly beliefs that by studying historical examples, both real and imagined, we can better identify and then critique the forces at work in contemporary culture—and, crucially for students at Georgia Tech— we can better create new tools and other technologies that will shape our digital future.

This approach, equal parts critical and creative, conceptual and applied, is most easily described by a term, "digital humanities," that has gained rapid currency in the academy (as well as in the *New York Times*) in the past few years. A term that once described the application of computational techniques to address traditional humanistic questions, digital humanities now encompasses the creation, application, and analysis of a wide range of media objects—from visualization software to videogames—as well as the study of how digital culture has, and will continue to shape humanities scholarship both inside and out of the academy.

In the lab I direct that bears that name, the Digital Humanities Lab, I aim to bring together students and faculty from across the Institute to explore the range of issues provoked, and practices generated, by our

I aim to bring togeth-
er students and faculty
from across the Institute
to explore the range of
issues provoked, and
practices generated,
by our present digital
mediascape.

present digital mediascape. Through the creation of software tools (and other digital methods) to support new forms of scholarship, and the support of digital projects prompted by new areas of research, we seek to explore questions of epistemology; or, as Joanna Drucker, a professor in the Department of Information Studies at UCLA, has described, "ways of thinking differently about how we know what we know, and how the interpretive task of the humanist is redefined" in the "changed conditions" of the digital age. At the DH Lab, our projects have ranged from the design of an interactive system for visualizing and exploring the themes contained within nineteenth century anti-slavery newspapers, to the deployment of techniques from the field of computational linguistics and information visualization in order to analyze the content of tens of thousands of letters written by (or to) Thomas Jefferson. In these projects, as in each project we undertake, we seek to synthesize cutting-edge computational techniques with the literary, historical, and cultural questions that drive humanities research.

In my courses, too, I bring together literary, historical, and cultural studies with applied media practice in order to allow students from far-ranging majors

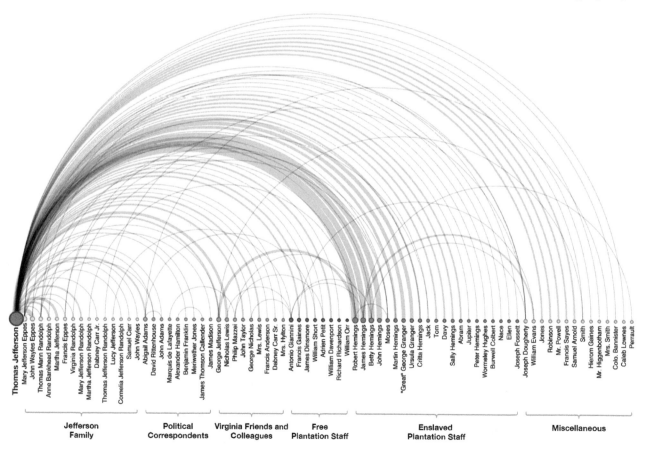

to express their own ideas and arguments about the topics under consideration. For a course that explored the idea of the archive, for instance, we began by asking general questions about why people keep things, how people keep things, and what to do about the things that, try as we may, we cannot keep at all. We examined theoretical formulations of—and challenges to—the concept of the archive through the lens of literary accounts of archives, as well as examples of archives, both print and digital, from the Georgia Tech and Emory library systems. After considering archives of documents and archives of junk, we then worked together as a class to design and implement a digital archive of materials from the Bud Foote Science Fiction Collection here at Georgia Tech.

In another course, centered on the idea of data, I asked my students to think about their SAT scores, their Facebook friends, and even their DNA, in order to understand how data structures their everyday lives. We traced the concept of data back to the Enlightenment, connecting eighteenth-century ideas about evidence and observation to examples, both historical and contemporary, that brought these concepts to the fore. After experimenting with a set of basic tools for data visualization, we created our own visualizations to offer comment on the long, fraught history of visual display.

My own research takes up these same topics. I am currently at work on a cultural history of data visualization, which traces the development of the visual display of quantitative information from the pioneering graphical charts created eighteenth-century political economists, to the schemes for visualizing history developed by nineteenth-century educators, and up through the present day—in the form of the visualizations and infographics found all over the web. Inspired by the increasing range of digital formats for publication, I am in the process of creating an online, image-based companion to what will become a scholarly book. In this way, the digital humanities function, for me, as both method and mission; as a way to engage with and offer comment on—in content and in form—the digital culture that informs and animates our everyday lives.

＊ ＊ ＊ ＊ ＊ ＊ ＊ ＊ ＊

# Kenneth Knoespel

# A Laboratory for the Future of Higher Education

A young woman entering Georgia Tech asked about majors. She had perfect SAT scores and said pointedly, 'Can you assure me that I won't waste either half of my brain?' This question is revealing because often Georgia Tech students think they must define themselves within a single field, limiting their strong desire to explore their intellectual creativity by bringing together multiple disciplines. For me the question emphasizes the crucial importance of LMC as an intellectual and creative setting enriched by the strengths of all of Georgia Tech.

Through the work of many colleagues and the steady support of Georgia Tech, LMC has become a laboratory for the emergence of curricula that integrates the humanities with science and technology. In 2003 the National Academy of Sciences recognized the important of our work, noting in Beyond Creativity: Technology, Innovation, and Creativity that "The success and prestige that the school enjoys within Georgia Tech and the new-media community at large have created visibility that would have been unavailable if it had remained a traditional English department. With the help of creative campaigning by the [LMC], the engineers and scientists of Georgia Tech, faculty members who hold the majority of clout within the university, have had little trouble understanding the benefits and advantages of a program in digital media."

Thomas Friedman reinforced the importance of Georgia Tech's evolving curriculum in *The World is Not Flat* (2006): "What the Georgia Tech model recognizes is that the world is increasingly going to be operating off the flat-world platform, with its tools for all kinds of horizontal collaboration." The rapid expansion of digital technology has reinforced the ways in which science and technology engages with other disciplines. Today LMC includes not only faculty with distinguished work in literature and film but faculty with degrees in Engineering and Computer Science who have chosen to shape new degree programs that integrate work in the humanities with digital media. The consequences of this integration for our work at Georgia Tech have been enormous. The French philosopher Bruno Latour has remarked that LMC has become an important laboratory for the future of education. Over the past ten years, our work has become a model for universities not only in the United States but in other countries. Together with the Ivan Allen College, we have been able to develop exchange programs and summer abroad programs in Asia, Europe, and South America

## LMC has become a laboratory for the emergence of curricula that integrates the humanities with science and technology.

When I arrived at Georgia Tech, I was using an IBM Selectric typewriter. Soon I had a dual-floppy IBM computer in my office. By 1989 I was using a GT-issued prototype laptop to transcribe Newton manuscripts at the Hebrew University in Jerusalem. I remember vividly the first e-mail I sent from my new home computer to a colleague at the university in 1987. I also remember the disbelief of aeronautical engineers when we presented 'a take-off and fly-away' of a helicopter on an Apple II computer rather than a Silicon Graphics machine. Together with colleagues, I learned that building degree programs that included applied work with computing and digital media enabled research that extended well beyond traditional boundaries in the humanities or social sciences.

Work at Georgia Tech has led to an undergraduate program in Computational Media and a graduate program in Digital Media that includes both a M.S. and Ph.D. A Bachelor of Science degree in Computational Media developed with the College of Computing has emphasized the importance of required courses in programming and the creative aspects of digital technology. The graduate program is recognized for its work in game development, augmented reality, digital theory, AI generated animation, interactive design, and Machinima. Nor do we forget our history: links between legacy media and dig-

ital media remain an important element in all the programs, as do the connections between humanities and science. The wildly successful Poetry@ Tech, inaugurated ten years ago by the American poet, Thomas Lux, has become recognized across the country. Supported by generous endowments from Henry Bourne and Bruce McEver, Poetry@ Tech reaches beyond the undergraduate and graduate programs to demonstrate how the study and the practice of poetry, often regarded as the core of the humanities, also works at the creative center of digital media.

Our collaborative educational laboratory is exemplified in the course on Global Issues and Leadership that I have developed with the head of the School of International Affairs. The course brings students in the humanities and social sciences together with students from across the campus. Together the students develop briefings on major social and political issues confronting the United States and the world. Chemical warfare, food deserts and obesity, the impacts of widening the Panama Canal, public education, digital security, and economic development in Africa have been among the projects presented. Each problem area has been presented to visiting leaders such as Senator Sam Nunn, Ambassador Andrew Young, Congressman John Lewis, Vice President of Coca-Cola Javier Goizueta, President and Executive Director of Georgia Public Broadcasting Teya Ryan, and President of the Georgia Partnership for Excellence in Education Steve Dolinger. Rather than focusing attention on a single discipline, the seminar stresses what is learned from applying the expertise of multiple disciplines to major problems confronting our societies. The course opens the artificial lines that often separate the humanities from other disciplines, and has reinforced the strength of Georgia Tech's Core Curriculum that requires all students to have competencies in math, science, and computing.

I developed another seminar, 'Witness to a Changing Conscience,' with GT Professor of Practice and Poetry@Tech visionary Bruce McEver, in which we explore the ways that major authors have documented changes in their thinking through their fiction and autobiographical work. Our students have considered Marcus Aurelius, Augustine, Montaigne, Jefferson, Emerson, Gandhi, Tolstoy, Martin Luther King, Thich Nhat Hanh, Flannery O'Connor, Orhan Pamuk. Recent visitors to the class include United States Presidential Medal of Freedom recipient Bill Foege, Harvard Divinity School Research Professor Harvey Cox, and the writer and journalist Tom Schachtman.

I have often described LMC as an archipelago of teaching and research. Richard Utz, our current chair, recognized the school's important work in Science Fiction by reminding us that we have become a Large Magellanic Cloud! The metaphor illustrates the importance of LMC's relations with disciplines across the Institute. We are hardly isolated and are vital to the very future of Georgia Tech. We are participating in building the new university by building a living laboratory for the future of education with colleagues across Georgia Tech. I'm proud that each student who joins us helps in building a new university.

• • • • • • • • • •

We are participating in building the new university by building a living laboratory for the future of education with colleagues across Georgia Tech. I'm proud that each student who joins us helps in building a new university.

"LMC research rocks! With an impressive number of National Science Foundation awards (four at last count) and support from the Gates Foundation and major corporations like Intel, LMC faculty and students are engaged in incredibly exciting interdisciplinary research projects with colleagues from across Georgia Tech. The efforts include improving STEM (science, technology, engineering, and math) education, focused efforts to improve the quality of life across the globe, advances in video game technology, and the creation of significant thought leadership platforms in film, digital media, and literature. Most of the research is showcased at student-led exhibitions each semester."

*Steve Cross,*
*GT Executive Vice-President*
*for Research*

**Brian Magerko**

# ADAM, EarSketch, and I

As both a cognitive scientist and a computer scientist, I have always been keenly interested in the formal representations of thought. Cognitive processes, knowledge, artificial intelligence—these are the phenomena that fascinate me.

What I had not noticed as a student was how consistently, when left to my own devices, my studies in cognition and computation veered off the steady path and swirled together in projects with a heavy humanities focus. Senior year: a robot comedy improv troupe; Advanced Artificial Intelligence (AI) course: a neural network for recognizing chorales written by J.S. Bach; dissertation work: an AI approach to creating interactive narratives.

There is a sublime beauty in the intersection between cognition and computation I had not realized in my early years. I had been too focused on games being the "it" medium in which to work, rather than looking at games—and digital media in general—as a means to an end—one of many trees in the forest. Three years into my career at Georgia Tech, when required to provide narrative to describe my career path for peer review, I had an opportunity to look beneath the surface and genuinely consider why I do what I do. Upon reflecting on my past and future work, it became obvious that creativity was the glue holding everything together: Understanding human creativity better, formally representing human creativity in computational systems, and supporting human creativity to support engagement and learning in digital media artifacts.

Creativity as a formal concept is the siren call of a phenomenon ridiculously hard to study and even harder to formally represent in computational systems. Still, creativity is one of those parts of the human experience that makes life so incredibly rich on a daily basis. It leads to surprise, to emotion, to connecting with others in a visceral and sacred way. It seems only natural to explore creativity as a first class phenomenon in the kinds of systems—cognitive systems—in which it exists. How are people creative? How can people be creative with computing to improve their cognition and learn? How can computers be creative? How can computers and humans be creative together to shape new creative paradigms and domains? Answering questions regarding the overlap between computing, cognition, and creativity is at the heart of the work we do in the Adaptive Digital Media (ADAM) Lab at Georgia Tech.

The research we engage in runs the spectrum from studying human creativity, creating computational representations of creative cognitive processes, to doing practice-based research that engages human creativity and cognition while becoming computationally literate. We study improvisational actors and pairs of people playing "pretend" as a way to better understand how people generate shared meaning together and how they collaboratively perform and unravel a story through their interactions over time. For example: We built a movement-installation piece built on the back of contemporary movement theory in dance and theater. And even our educational media work relies heavily on the potential of computing as a creative form to inspire and engage learners, like our EarSketch project described below.

EarSketch is one of the most surprising and oddly successful works to come out of the ADAM Lab. Rather than focusing on understanding human creativity to computationally represent it, this work engages learners in a creative practice—remixing music—by writing programming code. EarSketch is a multi-disciplinary research project, funded by the National Science Foundation, that explores how computational thinking can be taught through authentic artistic practices. We use computational music remixing (i.e., using code to manipulate loops, beats, and effects) as a means of captivating high school students' interest in traditional introductory computer science practices.

**EarSketch is a multi-disciplinary research project, funded by the National Science Foundation, that explores how computational thinking can be taught through authentic artistic practices.**

This involves a collaboration between academics; Atlanta high school teachers and policy makers; evaluators; and music industry professionals, such as Young Guru (Jay-Z's DJ and producer) and Richard Devine (internationally known electronic musician and sound designer).

The EarSketch environment consists of a Python code editing environment, a pedagogically appropriate Application Programming Interface (API) for remixing, a digital audio workstation, and a social media sharing site where students can share their projects and remix with each other's code. Students apply core computing concepts such as iteration, recursion, user-defined functions—in a domain that is both technical and expressive. And they learn basic aesthetic concepts in musical composition hand-in-hand with computing concepts.

This work has been piloted at multiple Atlanta-area schools and has been shown to both effectively teach computing principles as well as serve as a highly engaging learning domain for students who are traditionally underrepresented in computer science. It has also been used in an massively-online course on music technology, with over 10,000 students registered. While EarSketch has succeeded in teaching computing and increase student interest in computing as a discipline in general, success rates were even higher for underrepresented populations across gender and ethnicity. Women in particular are strongly motivated by the EarSketch experience and often change their attitudes about computing and their role in it.

EarSketch wants to offer an innovative, authentic learning experience for high school students that is both effective and appealing to students of different gender, ethnicity, and class backgrounds. We believe it has great potential to be used nationwide as a tool for learning computation and music technology. The curriculum and software are all freely available at http://earsketch.gatech.edu.

I would contend that EarSketch is the most symbolic work to come out of the ADAM lab in terms of showing the relevance of the arts and humanities to computing.  By tightly integrating music production and programming, computing becomes more relevant to learners, especially those who may be turned off by it otherwise.  There is something powerful about that combination that cannot be captured by music or programming alone; treating the computer as an expressive medium is as significant a mental turn as thinking of the typewriter as a medium for writing stories or canvas for painting.  Computing has the potential for being a new humanistic domain, in which creative practice involves computation as a way to communicate vision, as a collaborator, and as a means for forcing us to better understand ourselves, to formally consider why and how we engage in our various creative activities.

*Rapper, Young Guru with a student at Lanier High School Elementary, going over his EarSketch assignment.*

"I do not want to imagine a world of future business leaders who cannot communicate, who cannot critically evaluate evidence, who cannot consider the implications of technology, who cannot construct and make meaning from interactions, who cannot understand our cultural embeddedness. Thanks to LMC, I don't have to imagine this scenario for the Scheller College of Business graduates. They learn a broad mindset from their LMC classes that enables them to see a different view of humanity, and its interface with technology. Their perspective, and our future, is enhanced for the better because they learn in and out of classes with LMC majors."

*Terry Blum, Director, GT Institute for Leadership and Entrepreneurship; Tedd Munchak Chair & Professor, Scheller College of Business*

# Carol Senf

# Why We Need the Gothic in a Technological World

Living in a world that purports to value scientific predictability while teaching (for 32 years) at an engineering school, it's sometimes hard to justify why I value the Gothic and argue that it is even more essential today.

It's not because I'm besotted by tradition though I am fond of the architecture often described as Gothic. Originally built in Europe between the 12th and the 16th centuries and later revived in the 19th, Gothic architecture is identified by the ribbed vault and the flying buttress, both of which allowed for dramatic interior spaces that are literally filled with light. Think Notre Dame in Paris, the York Minster, or Westminster Abbey. Of course, one need not go to Europe for a Gothic fix: the architect who designed the Tech Tower and its sister buildings at Agnes Scott and Clemson echoed the aspiration evident in medieval Gothic, as did the architect for the postmodern building on West Peachtree formerly known as the IBM Building.

However, Gothic or The Gothic is associated with other arts as well. Not only does Gothic refer to an extinct Germanic language, but it also characterizes several kinds of script or typography: 1) A script used in Western Europe from approximately 1150 into the 17th century, and 2) sans-serif typography, such as Ariel or Helvetica, often used for dramatic headings. And to make matters even more complicated, there's also Gothic music, a type of rock and roll, and Gothic clothing—think Wynona Ryder in *Beetlejuice* or almost anything by Tim Burton.

While I'm fond of Gothic architecture, having never met a Gothic cathedral I didn't like, and use Gothic type regularly, they aren't what I think of when I argue that the Gothic is essential in the modern technological world. Indeed the Gothic as I see it encompasses some of the previous examples I noted, being a way of describing (or attempting to describe) or responding to a world that cannot be fully explained by science or mathematics, a world that is large enough to include the mysterious, the liminal, and the terrible.

The Gothic as a way of seeing the world originated at the end of the eighteenth century, when a sense of scientific certainty was beginning to emerge. I suspect that the Gothic was, even then, a counterbalance produced by writers and thinkers who felt limited by such a confident worldview and recognized that the power of the past, the irrational, and the violent continues to hold sway in the world. Two hundred (and more) years later, there's much that science cannot explain and problems that technology cannot solve. Some days it's easy to feel paralyzed by forces beyond our comprehension and beyond our control.

To get a handle on the Gothic, it helps to go back to what is arguably the first "modern" example, Horace Walpole's 1764 novel, *The Castle of Otranto*, which he subtitled "A Gothic Story." Walpole noted that he wanted to combine elements of the medieval romance, which he found too fanciful, and the modern novel, which he believed was limited by the very ordinariness of realism. Hence he invented an antiquarian who discovered the fragments of an ancient manuscript and set it in a medieval castle. That manuscript tells of a villainous aristocrat who will do anything to gain power and of several persecuted female characters who attempt to elude his control. Writers, filmmakers, and video game designers often adapt these conventions. Thus we have come to expect persecuted heroines, inscrutable villains, supernatural forces, and decaying medieval structures in works described as Gothic.

An easy formula to adapt, one might say, but the Gothic has been well adapted by Mary Shelley (*Frankenstein*), the Brontes (*Jane Eyre, Wuthering Heights*, and *The Tenant of Wildfell Hall*), Henry James (*The Turn of the Screw*) and Bram Stoker (*Dracula*), not to mention Poe, Faulkner, and Ste-

phen King many of whom adapt the conventions to explore their own worlds and add a convention (that of multiple narrators as if to remind readers that no single human being has the whole truth).

Stoker brings a monstrous figure from the medieval past to London, the heart of Empire. Juxtaposing past and present, Stoker opposes this figure with everything that modern science and law have to offer—the power of combination—and tracks Dracula to his Transylvanian lair, the very name "beyond the forest" evoking mystery. Using the tools of Empire, the kukri knife and the Bowie knife, Stoker's "Crew of Light" seems to destroy Dracula, and a brief epilogue shows them seven years later at the site of their victory. However, the easy victory fails to satisfy. Readers may remember

> **The Gothic as a way of seeing the world originated at the end of the eighteenth century, when a sense of scientific certainty was beginning to emerge.**

Van Helsing's observation that nothing manufactured by human beings could destroy the vampire, and evidence from the manuscript suggests that Stoker contemplated destroying Dracula's castle at his death, but someone—Stoker or an editor—excised the paragraph in which the castle is destroyed. Having the vast ruined castle loom over the human characters is somehow more satisfying, as it suggests that the mysterious forces Dracula represents by are somehow more powerful than contemporary science and technology, which often fail despite the smug self-assurance of both scientists and representatives of the legal system.

## Students "get" Stoker's message about the limitations of science. Scientists and programmers, Tech students know there are things they do not understand and over which they have no control.

Students "get" Stoker's message about the limitations of science. Scientists and programmers, Tech students know there are things they do not understand and over which they have no control. Much as they want easy answers, they see complexity around them. Emphasizing multiplicity and complexity is what Gothic does best. Because I see my job as reinforcing that suspicion of easy "one size fits all" solutions, I believe that the Gothic is essential to our technological world.

"**A master's or doctoral degree in LMC's Digital Media program opens a unique set of career pathways, for people who want to design the future, not just have it come at them.**"

*Susan E. Cozzens,*
*GT Vice Provost for Graduate Education*
*& Faculty Affairs*

# Michael Nitsche

# What I Make

Somewhat hidden away on the top floor of the Student Center at Georgia Tech is the craft center. The size of a large classroom, it features some pottery wheels, shelves, paints and brushes, tools, workbenches, but no computer, screen, or projector in the main area. The doing, at least here, is physical. You come in, put on an apron, collect your tools, and sit on the wheel. It is a great place to work on media.

Stuff and its making is personal matter. We build not only a frame for a house to have a sheltering roof but also one for ourselves to define who we are—willingly or utterly unaware of the consequences. This equally applies to digital artifacts but it becomes evermore complicated when those artifacts are procedural machines themselves. Whether we build a digital media artifact—like an interface, a video game, a 3D world, a web site—or whether we use one—play a game, surf the web, text on a cell phone—the action is a defining one not only for the digital world but also for us, as we are constantly recreating ourselves anew through it. What creative practices make up these actions and how can we claim them—or in some cases re-claim them from legal or technological straight jackets—back for the human who makes the action and herself through it?

In today's globalized economies craft is a marginal player. Making your own mug might very well be more expensive than buying an imported one. It probably will be more flawed and it certainly will take more time. As commercially viable production, craft is hard to sustain. Leaning on craft is also not treading a way back to Ruskin-infused utopias of yesterday. There is no step out of a mediated society, which is why we need every help we can find to live within it. Sidestepping the vocabulary and practices of "virtual" digital media by focusing on the wet clay spinning under your hands is not a revivalist rejection but a gesture of reclaiming and recontextualizing. From a design perspective, it supports the realization that our actions are never virtual but remain constructions of self and others. From a technological perspective, it emphasizes the "physical" and the "things" in expanding fields such as physical computing and the Internet of Things.

At the far end of the Ferst Center, not too far from the craft shop, a second place deals with this challenge in its own way. Georgia Tech's black box theater is the home to DramaTech and lays claim to be the longest continuously running theater in Atlanta. Whenever possible, I take my students for at least one session per term into the black box. At times we awkwardly play between the set pieces of some stage production or present our concepts and ideas literally from a stage using props for an upcoming musical. We have conducted Improv exercises, dance workshops, puppetry rehearsals, cell phone theater, among other things—all in pursuit of digital media design.

Performance is production like crafting, but of expression. It is a form of making and setting a frame. The black box is not only an inspirational place, it is also a testing ground for the performance of self that digital media inherently include. Theater, much like craft, is largely seen as a niche media, surpassed long time ago by film, television, and video games. Yet, once again, the turn to performance is not a revisionist step back but a necessary move forward as the digital transcends our everyday life. Pressing a button on the keyboard at our working desk, looking at the screen of a cell phone during a bus ride, and being motion captured by a game console as we exercise in our living room—these are relevant actions not only for the digital device but also for our surroundings. They make the spaces not only in the virtual worlds they are read into, but also in the physical worlds where they originate.

Because digital media remains a developing field where new challenges rise seemingly with the cycles of next gen game consoles and smartphones, we need spaces like craft shops and theater stages. They are practical workshops for creative activity that is at the heart of our interaction with digital stuff. My work as a digital media designer is explorative as it tries to grow with the field. To do so, it builds on those spaces of practice. Explorative means that it develops prototypes and classes that help us to ask new questions, instead of teaching pre-conceived answers. Exploration means that we produce analyses of the existent mediascapes as well as relevant questions to challenge them—in theory and practice. The shop and the stage are two locations that help us to do exactly that.

# Jay David Bolter

# Examining and Changing a World of Media

We live in a world of media, especially digital media, and the changes in the ways we use media constitute one of the major cultural stories of the past half century. The developments in the 1970s and 1980s (cable television, VCRs, CDs, desktop computers and then laptops, and computer communication mediated by modems) were followed by videogames, the introduction of cellphones, the World Wide Web, and the explosive spread of the Internet in the 1990s, and then by smart phones and social media in the 2000s. All but the poorest among us have cell phones, and the use of computers and the Internet for entertainment and social communication now rivals or surpasses commercial and business uses. According to a study in 2011, nearly 30% of all Internet traffic into the American home in the evenings is accounted for by Netflix and other streaming films and television services. Because these media surround us, it is easy to ignore the prominent role they now play in our lives. Because young people have grown up with so many media devices and services, and their parents have grown old with them, it is easy to forget how much our media landscape has changed in the past 50 years.

If we could somehow transport an American through time from 1960 to 2010, she would have little trouble adapting to everyday life and little reason to be surprised, except in the crucial areas of media and communications. As she walked along the streets, she would be puzzled to see many of the passers-by holding miniature walky-talkies to their ears or tapping on tiny keyboards and screens, while many others appeared to be listening to music through headphones attached to tiny transistor radios. If she walked into an office building, she would be struck by all the individual computer consoles with videoscreens, which have not only replaced typewriters on the secretaries' desks, but found their way to the desks of technical workers and even executives, who never typed their own letters in the 1960s. If she visited a home, she would find more computers—in a father's or mother's home office, in the children's bedrooms, and perhaps even in the kitchen. Occasionally she might find the family watching television together, but it could now be an enormous flat-screen television of astonishing clarity with hundreds of channels as well as instant access to films and whole television series, streaming from yet another computer. More often, she would find various family members using their own media devices, and she would notice that the children were ap-

If we could somehow transport an American through time from 1960 to 2010, she would have little trouble adapting to everyday life and little reason to be surprised [...]

parently typing messages to one friend on the same computer or tablet with which they were talking to another. A few years after our time traveler left, Stanley Kubrik's epic film *2001* (1968) would have shown her an astronaut making a video phone call (handled by AT&T) back to earth. By 2010, though, everyone seemed to be able to use their small computer screens to talk to and view each other, and their video camera, embedded at the top of the screen, was like a tiny version of HAL's oculus.

Perhaps nothing in our culture today would mystify a visitor from 1960 more than social media such as Twitter, YouTube, and Facebook. These forms of expression have analogies in practices that she knew (writing letters and greeting cards, making home movies or audio cassettes, pasting travel photos into albums as keepsakes and to inflict on friends and neighbors), but their technical configuration and their manic attraction for tens of millions of Americans and hundreds of millions of people around the world would have been unimaginable in 1960.

If we tried to sum up the changes in two words, they would be "ubiquity" and "diversity." All sorts of media products and services are available everywhere, for a price, and, despite the predictions, all these products and services have not melted into a single universal form. Charting these changes and considering their meaning for our current cultural moment is the task of the discipline called "media studies." And it is one of the disciplines that we practice here in Literature, Media, and Communication (LMC).

As valuable as media studies is, however, it can only provide us with a clearer understanding of the history that has led to our current cultural moment.

The exciting next step is to take an active role in shaping the future of media. That task belongs to the Digital Media program in LMC, where faculty members, graduate students, and undergraduates create and test prototypes for new digital media forms. These experiments draw on our understanding of the origins of digital media and the relationship to the important forms of the past (such as film, television, and the printed book). But they also explore the qualities of digital media that distinguish them from their predecessors, such as interactivity and procedurality.

For example, I work in the Augmented Environments Lab (AEL) with colleagues and students to design new forms of entertainment and informal education using the technologies of augmented and mixed reality. Imagine that you are walking down historic Auburn Avenue in Atlanta, Georgia. "Sweet Auburn" was the center of African-American culture during the first half of the 20th century. Your smart phone can be your guide, providing stories about the musicians, preachers, businessmen, and civil-rights activists as you pass by the buildings where they lived and worked. You can see photos of the Royal Peacock club from the 1940s, superimposed on the current building, and hear the music of Duke Ellington, who played there. The voice that accompanies you on your walk is that of Andrew Young, one-time mayor of Atlanta and an activist who worked with Martin Luther King. This is the kind of experience that we are creating in the AEL. Such experiences are not only experiments with a new technology, although it is great fun to put these new mobile devices with high-quality graphics, cameras, orientation and positioning sensors through their paces. Our experiences also depend on the lessons in design and media studies that we draw from looking at our rich media heritage of the

**"LMC research and teaching encompass a world of literature, media, and communication!  Remarkable are the scope and depth of work in computing and digital design, gender and race, film, performance, and science fiction.  LMC defines what it means for faculty and students to take humanistic perspectives in a technological universe!"**

Mary Frank Fox, Advance Professor,
GT School of Public Policy;
Co-Director: Center of the Study of Women,
Science, and Technology

# T. Hugh Crawford

# Making Theory: Useless Design/Risky Pedagogy

As a technological institution, the Georgia Institute of Technology embraces design studios as fundamental to its pedagogical mission. In my work teaching the humanities at Tech, I make a serious effort to incorporate some design practices into classes, helping the students understand the complexity that making entails but also to build on the learning that making produces. Put simply, a student who has squared a round timber with broadax and adze has a different understanding of the second chapter of Thoreau's *Walden* than the casual reader.

I use the term "Useless Design" to designate a pedagogical practice where the product being designed has little or no inherent economic or instrumental value, and the primary skills involved in its production will not likely be useful in a student's academic or professional career. Learning the basics of blacksmithing or timber-framing does not generally lead to professionally useful skills for a Georgia Tech graduate. Instead, my purpose is to get students to become attentive, to think deeply about processes, to reflect on why they do the things they do, rather than measuring their success by making a practical application. This is where my approach diverges from many of the Georgia Tech design practices which are concerned with bringing a useful device or application to market. Useless Design helps students slow down, focus on and articulate both the familiar and the unfamiliar parts of making. Useless practices prompt naive questioning that probes historical circumstances and social norms, and helps develop a humanistic perspective on a technological world. By recasting technology as a set of practices that must be learned and articulated through an historically sedimented space, I try to foreground making as a process that draws across many disciples and blurs most of those disciplinary boundaries.

David Pye, design theorist and master woodworker, makes a distinction between what he calls the workmanship of certainty and that of risk. Although he does not privilege one term over the other, he makes an effort to draw out the positive value a workmanship of risk can produce. Briefly, a workmanship of certainty involves the use of uniform materials and a highly regulated set of tools (tools that minimize an operator's mistakes or variations). A workmanship of risk, on the other hand, deploys non-uniform mate-

rials with generally unregulated tools, demanding of the worker careful attention through each step, an intimate understanding of both material and tool, and an awareness of ongoing and impending failure. Such workers approach the task with care and humility, and never stop learning from the material, the tools, and the practice. To paraphrase George Sturt, they must become "friends, as only a craftsman can be, with timber and iron. The grain of wood [tells] secrets to them." Pye's notion of the workmanship of risk helps define a pedagogy of risk, one where the final products are not clear, nor is the path to get there obvious. A pedagogically risky class approaches assignments with care, humility, and openness. It recognizes that the class, its projects and its practices must also be designed in an iterative process. The work is open-ended and exploratory: assignments, competencies, and labor are renegotiated and redistributed constantly, while all materials, tools, and practices are carefully questioned and historically situated. As the philosopher Martin Heidegger argues, risk discloses new worlds.

**Crafting Learning:**

"Freshman Composition (1102)." The subject was the history of trees—primarily as commodities. After a series of readings and several paper assignments, the students decided to collaborate on a project focusing on the history of building practices, skill acquisition, and the role of modeling in knowledge production. They built three slices of a building that could be assembled into a small playhouse (not completely useless) via three teams: one researched 19th century building and made a timber-framed "bent," one did 20th century building with dimensional lumber, and the last did 21st

> [...] a student who has squared a round timber with broadax and adze has a different understanding of the second chapter of Thoreau's Walden than the casual reader.

century building with plywood "slot and tab" techniques cut out on a large CNC machine. They made hand drawn plans, CADed plans, 3D printed or laser cut small scale models, and full scale section models. At the same time they developed a set of learning objectives, and produced a series of exhibition materials including an illustrated magazine on the history of timber-framing, dimensional lumber construction, and the history of plywood and CNC production. They wrote essays on modeling, design and "learning by doing," and made animated GIFs of CADed plans, videos showing building, posters on history of materials, and, of course, a web page.

"Major Author Seminar: Herman Melville's *Moby-Dick* and 19th Century Technology." Students read the novel as an encyclopedia of 19th century technology, with each producing a research project on the relation of that technology to 21st century practices. In addition, they chose several technol-

**After reading Thoreau's masterpiece,** *Walden,* **the class proceeded to frame up a full scale version of his house using only the tools he could have used: axes, adzes, chisels, and hand-saws (no power tools).**

ogies to understand through "hands-on learning" including rope production, knot tying, celestial navigation, candle production, blacksmithing (they forged a harpoon on an anvil), and a 22 ft. plywood model of a whale skeleton cut on a CNC machine eventually donated to a south Atlanta nature center.

"Major Author Seminar: Henry David Thoreau." After reading Thoreau's masterpiece, *Walden,* the class proceeded to frame up a full scale version of his house using only the tools he could have used: axes, adzes, chisels, and hand-saws (no power tools). They went to the woods, chopped down trees, squared them with broad axes, and framed up the building. They also wrote essays, made a documentary film, and presented their research at several scholarly conferences.

Each of these projects' uselessness is their greatest asset (e.g., the harpoon will thankfully never strike a whale). Instead, the students questioned each step in their processes, discussed at length any design proposal, and constantly reframed forms of medi-

ation and the goals of their research. They learned that all materials—wood, paper, 3D printing, iron, words, etc.—are recalcitrant, and that making involves both designing objects and designing learning.

# Qi Wang

# Mapping Cinema and the World

Our current globalizing world is experiencing an unprecedented rate and scale of technological development and media updating. With Twitter or Facebook friends, familiar or new, in America or Asia, broadcasting diverse daily lives and sharing links to unimagined information, how might an individual brace against this overwhelming wave of information without getting swept away and losing a sense of time, identity, and direction in life in the act of easy connecting? Other than the necessary technical knowledge of codes and skills, how might a student—as a young person with much potential and promise that needs to be tapped carefully and wisely—learn to emerge out of that ocean of information and demand in order to become an ably equipped navigator of contemporary life, not merely as a user, consumer or tourist but more as an informed traveller and a capable creator of good technologies? The latter image, in my understanding, is what the official strategic plan of Georgia Tech identifies as one of our five goals: graduating "good global citizens."

With its necessary combination of arts and technologies, the field of cinema and media studies is doubtless a highly productive place for the education of students as intelligent citizens capable of seeing through films and other cultural products as complex artifacts involving not only technology and industry but also culture and politics. On one hand, students are exposed to the most famous and aesthetically accomplished films and directors from all over the world. They learn the essential terminology/technology—e.g., narrative, mise-en-scène, cinematography, and editing—whose varied uses have created such fascinating yet diverse styles by directors like Alfred Hitchcock, Akira Kurosawa, Michelangelo Antonioni, Yimou Zhang, and others. On the other hand, they explore questions like: why did the genre of film noir—with its nights, shadows, and rainy streets even when set in Los Angeles—happen to reach its fullest development at no other historical moment than the mid-to-late 1940s? Why in Hitchcock's stories of murder do we tend to find images of an eye, a whirlpool, a man who knows too much and a woman who knows even better? What kind of culturally and/or historically specific understanding of architecture, space and existence lies in the long takes of Antonioni (Italy), the grid-like formal structure in Yasujiro Ozu (Japan), and the unforgettable choreography of colors in Yimou Zhang (China)? How and why did a certain director and/with a certain style happen to take form at a certain moment in world history? Obviously, questions like these demand an understanding of not only the textual details of a film, a director or a genre but also the contextual factors that informed their birth and growth. Through such guiding and training practices in the analysis and ap-

preciation of films as organic products of culture and history, it is my goal to cultivate in the students an augmented sensitivity for form and beauty, an enriching curiosity for the fuller pictures of phenomena (whether cultural, social or natural), and a deep desire and respect for what one does not yet know or know fully enough.

As a member of the film faculty in LMC, I both teach general film courses and specialize in East Asian film studies. Whether speaking about Chinese martial arts cinema, or world-famous filmmakers from East Asia, or the theoretical (yet also highly applicable) subject of space and place in cinema and media, I am committed to cultivating in the students a sense of comfort, confidence, and curiosity for non-Western cultural contents, forms, and patterns. Whether from East or West, the young adults of Georgia Tech deserve to be exposed to the very best. Wherever their home country is (though understandably with the majority from the US), the students of Georgia Tech are being prepared and encouraged to be at home in the world, being able to actively participate in its continual development as well-informed, well-prepared and healthily motivated insiders.

With that universalist educational goal in mind, in my various courses on East Asian and world cinema I tend to adopt a comparative approach. For example, in my Martial Arts Cinema course, I provide a survey of the history and theory of Chinese martial arts cinema and its international extrapolations in the context of transnational cinema. While it focuses on representative films, directors and performers from Mainland China, Taiwan, and Hong Kong in a largely chronological framework, it also introduces samples from Japan, South Korea, and the U.S.. For their projects students are encouraged to bring in relevant examples from any national cinema.

I also teach Space in Cinema and Media, a course specifically developed with the goal of inspiring students to think and explore their actual relationship with the world, which ranges from their current position at Georgia Tech near downtown Atlanta, their daily environment saturated with entertainment and social media as well as educational technologies, to their imagined or tentatively constructed relationship with other places, cultures, and histories, etc.. That course uses examples from cinema and introduce students to contemporary theories of spatiality. The students and I consider

> **Wherever their home country is (though understandably with the majority from the US), the students of Georgia Tech are being prepared and encouraged to be at home in the world [...]**

the architectural, aesthetic, historical, narrative, physical, psychological, philosophical, social, and symbolic dimensions of the course subject, and examine how these might be mobilized productively to understand and describe space, its functions in cinema and media, and ways in which we as spectators, users, and critical subjects can relate to and learn from all those things.

As I have emphasized to the students in the classroom, I hope they will take the knowledge and questions thus learned and raised, continuing onto their own journey in education, work and life as curious, informed, and brave travelers. In their navigation through the competing allures and demands in life, I hope they will be able to create a most enriching itinerary or pattern—the map of their life—along which they are able to relate and contribute to the world and live their lives to the fullest.

*President Dr. G.P. "Bud" Peterson getting oriented
at the Center by LMC's Karen Head*

# Karen Head

# At the Center: Innovation in Research, Practice, and Service for 21st Century "Writing Centers"

In the 1970's a new unit began appearing in American universities: the Writing Center. These units were created to offer supplemental academic resources and tutoring for students who wanted to improve their writing. For many of the founding scholars, writing centers were designed to places that would support the interdisciplinary study of writing—places that could transcend departmental boundaries. Creating such spaces was also an attempt to transcend misguided ideas about what traditional English departments do; they are much more than places where students learn to write college essays. These early scholars wanted to raise standards of and provide support for a variety of discourse communities throughout their institutions, offering "safe spaces" within which anyone could explore ways to become a better communicator. These safe spaces were designed to encourage frank discussions about rhetoric and composition across disciplines without connecting it to the harsher criticism of formal evaluation. In other words, these were places staffed by people who were not responsible for awarding grades, but instead focused on the higher goal of leading discussions about the importance of excellent communication for any purpose.

Unfortunately, the faculty, staff, students and administrators at many institutions considered writing centers to be mostly about remediation: places bad writers were sent to be "fixed." While some people still believe such centers are only about remediation, we are pleased that the culture at Georgia Tech is helping subvert this notion: ours is a place where the best students come to become even better. Since our founding and my appointment as director of the Communication Center in 2011, my charge is to make our center a benchmark for writing center research, pedagogy and practice—a place that returns to the ideal of a safe space for active debate and discourse about the best ways to communicate in a variety of modes.

While our center is relatively new, the commitment to such work can be traced back nearly forty years when one of the first female instructors at Georgia Tech, Helen Naugle, co-opted an empty classroom and began tutoring students in writing. As an engineering school, our students have often lacked excellent communication skills, so it is no surprise that Professor Naugle was looking for ways to supplement traditional classroom instruction. The seeds Naugle planted would take years to blossom, but she inspired conversations about founding a writing center at Georgia Tech that continued until her dream became my reality.

As part of the innovative Clough Undergraduate Learning Commons, ours is a center granted a prime location with state-of-the-art technology and budgetary support from the central administration. Historically, many writing centers have been located in remote or undesirable spaces. Our dean, Dr. Jacqueline Royster, tells the story from early in her career when she opened a center in an old storage closet behind a campus snack bar. My first day in our multimodal communication center (we now help students negotiate communication in a variety of modes, not just for writing), I was so overwhelmed by the potential of what we would be able to do with students that I wandered around the space in awe—finally retreating to my office, collapsing in my chair, and weeping joyfully. Here was a space designed for students, and I was keenly aware of its special nature. Our students would benefit from a center full of all the bells and whistles—it has everything that writing center directors wish for but rarely have: SmartBoards, video-capture and video-conferencing equipment, computer stations, scanners, iPads, and even a 3D printer. Our students also benefit from our ability to provide the very best tutoring staff; it is rare to have a sizeable professional staff of postdoctoral fellows who split time between teaching in the LMC writing program and tutoring in the center.

Another part of our mission is to find ways to encourage students to become part of our community of learners and scholars. Foremost we want to disabuse students that our center is a last resort for the struggling. We want them to understand that this is place where exciting things happen, where even our best students come to hone their projects. Our work touches every aspect of life at Georgia Tech, whether helping students prepare research papers or

**While some people still believe such centers are only about remediation, we are pleased that the culture at Georgia Tech is helping subvert this notion: ours is a place where the best students come to become even better.**

presentations, make documentary films, develop scientific documents for the public, write novels, or master the art of public speaking. Communication is a fundamental component for success, and our center's mission is to help our students master the competencies they will need to be successful in their academic and professional lives.

From an everyday perspective, writing center work is about having meaningful conversations: tutors and students talking about the best way(s) to communicate an idea. Technological tools can help make those conversations more productive, even more efficient, but it is the conversations that continue to matter most. From these conversations we also form many of our research questions and projects. Our professional staff members are already acknowledged as award-winning tutors as well as significant contributors in research journals and at research conferences. Additionally, we involve students in our research. In fact, some of the students who work in our center (as peer-tutors or as research assistants) have engaged in important research they have presented at prestigious academic conferences.

In the last few years, conversations about higher education have often focused on questions about efficiency. As we turn toward technology for answers, we must also ask important questions about what our students might gain or lose from the changes we implement. Certainly we want to offer the best educational resources to the greatest number of students. The Communication Center at Georgia Tech is committed to innovation in teaching and learning, and because we are fortunate enough to have "all the bells and whistles" we are positioned uniquely to pursue research that will help shape the ways writing centers are designed or redesigned, and the best outcome is that our students are the primary beneficiaries of this work.

• • • • • • • • •

Another part of our mission is to find ways to encourage students to become part of our community of learners and scholars. Foremost we want to disabuse students that our center is a last resort for the struggling.

Lisa Yaszek

# Amazing Stories, or, Why We Do Science Fiction at Georgia Tech

In 1926 Luxembourgian-American inventor Hugo Gernsback published the first issue of *Amazing Stories*, a magazine that would go on to inspire the millions of books, films, graphic novels, and video games we now describe as "science fiction." Indeed, Gernsback was so passionate about this new mode of storytelling that he prophesied it would be "an important factor in making the world a better place to live in… educating the public to the possibilities of science and the influence of science on life…. If every man, woman, boy, and girl could be induced to read science fiction right along, there would certainly be a great resulting benefit to the community. Science fiction would make them happier, give them a broader understanding of the world, make them more tolerant."

I often wish I had a time machine to go back to 1926 and talk with Gernsback about the similarities between his dream and Georgia Tech's mission to solve twenty-first century problems by innovating at the intersection of science, technology, and the arts. Better yet, I'd bring him forward in time to see how many of us are contributing to that mission today by engaging with science fiction across media. I think he would be tickled pink—but not surprised—to learn about all the different ways we use science fiction as a focusing lens to examine the world's most pressing scientific and social issues and to imagine better futures for all. As we like to say here in LMC, science fiction is a truly global language that allows people to communicate their experiences with science and technology across centuries, continents, and cultures.

The notion that science fiction is a global language drives all my research activities. For instance, in *The Self-Wired: Technology and Subjectivity in Contemporary Narrative*, I explore how authors and filmmakers we don't associate with science fiction use characters such as "the cyborg" and story types such as "the utopia" to make sense of changing relations between science, society, and the self. In a related vein, my book *Galactic Suburbia: Recovering Women's Science Fiction* shows how women writing science fiction after World War II used their chosen genre to contribute to culture-wide debates about women's work as homemakers, activists, scientists, and artists—and how, in doing so, they changed the face of science fiction forever. Consider, for instance, Steven Spielberg's *Jurassic Park*: In the middle of the movie the female lead turns to a male scientist

**Of course, science fiction isn't just for faculty at Georgia Tech. Rather, our students are partners in wonder who help us develop clearer pictures of science fiction as the premiere story form of modernity.**

and says "the only thing that matters now is family." As a science fiction fan, I can't help but think the only thing that would really matter in that situation would be getting away from the human-eating dinosaurs. But ever since I wrote *The Self-Wired* and *Galactic Suburbia*, I've also been able to appreciate how Spielberg draws on the history of the genre he loves to get viewers thinking about the impact of science and technology on our most fundamental social units. And so by doing science fiction studies, I get to double my pleasure in science fiction stories themselves.

Another reason I do science fiction studies is that I get to use my expertise to collaborate with colleagues across disciplines. A few years ago I worked on a National Science Foundation grant with two public policy professors and a nanoscientist to determine how new ideas about nanotechnology circulate through the American imagination. Initially we assumed that scientists develop these new ideas, public policy makers create laws that regulate their application, and then finally writers and filmmakers "translate" them for the public. Much to my delight, however, we learned that we had it backward:

authors have been speculating about the possibilities inherent in small-scale engineering ever since Jonathan Swift published *Gulliver's Travels* in the eighteenth century, while scientists and public policymakers have, since the middle of the twentieth century, shaped their own ideas about this subject in relation to science fiction! It was an exciting insight that made us realize science fiction is a lot like oxygen: invisible, everywhere around us, and something we breathe in without a second thought.

Of course, science fiction isn't just for faculty at Georgia Tech. Rather, our students are partners in wonder who help us develop clearer pictures of science fiction as the premiere story form of modernity. For instance, I begin my class on global science fiction with a brief history of American science fiction. I then draw on my own research to show students how African-American and women writers have generated their own rich traditions of speculative fiction, thereby challenging the clichéd belief that science fiction is "just about white boys and their toys." After students learn about American science fiction, they team up to research and teach their own units on science fiction around the world. This is my favorite part of the class because I get to learn so much. Did you know that South American authors have been writing science fiction since the 1830s? Or that manga was a trivial art form in Japan until the government partnered with artists to export it to the United States in the 1980s? Or that the 2011 science fiction-superhero film *Ra-One* holds the record for the largest international theatrical release of an Indian film? Neither did I—until my students unearthed these facts. As it turns out, the story of science fiction is even more, well, amazing than I thought.

Finally, as my students and I like to remind people, science fiction is both serious work and serious fun. We aim to convey this message to both the greater Georgia Tech and the greater science fiction communities with our Sci Fi Radio Lab, a variety program dedicated to "the best in everything science fiction" that airs on WREK 91.1, Georgia Tech's student-run radio station, every Thursday at 7 pm EST. The mad labsters, as I like to call them, engage in a variety of on-air activities that include interviewing science fiction artists, producing science fiction dramas, and developing original segments such as "two minute madness," where listeners have—you guessed it, two minutes—to weigh in on the topic of the week. We also celebrate the joy of science fiction through community collaborations such as our current Rite of Passage project, in which we are partnering with local media companies to produce the first ever full-length African American alternate history film. This project enables Georgia Tech students, staff, and faculty members to get involved in every aspect of independent filmmaking, from fund raising and location scouting to costume design and acting. Taken together, these research, teaching, and production activities illustrate how

we here at Georgia Tech are realizing Hugo Gernsback's dream of using science fiction to build a happier, more equitable, and more enlightened world.

● ● ● ● ● ● ● ● ● ●

My students and I like to remind people, science fiction is both serious work and serious fun. We aim to convey this message to both the greater Georgia Tech and the greater science fiction communities.

# Janet Murray

# Inventing the Medium:
# The Radical Challenge of
# Humanistic Digital Design

We live at an extraordinary time in human history when a new medium of representation has come into our hands. This has happened before—most spectacularly in the unrecorded moment when our early human ancestors invented spoken language, and again with the invention of drawing, writing, printing, photography, and the diverse electronic recording and transmitting media of the past two centuries: the telegraph, telephone, movies, radio, and television. The computer, like all of these media, is a means of focusing shared attention by establishing conventions for capturing information in a commonly shared code and moving it across time and space. And like earlier media, it is transformative because of its augmentation of our powers to share our thoughts and coordinate our behaviors.

As a humanist trained in the history of the novel, I was drawn to the then nameless profession of interaction design when I was teaching at MIT in the early 1980s and my students showed me the first interactive narrative artifacts ever made—a text-based conversation named Eliza that responded like a therapist by echoing keywords taken from the user's input ("Tell me more about your mother.") and a text-based adventure game called Zork that put the player in a navigable maze with trolls and treasures ("A passage leads to the west and a dark staircase can be seen leading upward"). I had learned programming working for IBM between college and graduate school and so I understood how these interactive stories could be made of computer code. I realized from studying the development of the English novel that expressive new conventions of storytelling could grow over time within a tradition of practice. It was exciting to me that my students and I could help to build this tradition of practice by making narratives out of code. And as a humanist I also wanted to describe the tradition, to write books and articles about it as well as to make artifacts. Since the 1980s, I have seen both practices grow and cross-fertilize one another: the design work of inventing new expressive and informational digital genres, and the analytical work of describing these new artifacts as part of larger cultural practices.

The boundary between videogames and stories has proven to be a particularly fertile expanse, with many kinds of practitioners, some more literary and text-based, some more cinematic, some more mainstream and formulaic, some more independent and idiosyncratic. Humanistic discourse has had to expand just as it did with the advent of film to consider games as complex cultural forms worthy of analysis. Designers have welcomed this discourse as a source of vocabulary for describing what they do, helping them to articulate their aesthetics, and to identify ways to do it better.

Faculty and students in Digital Media at Georgia Tech occupy a privileged position as both theorists and practitioners of digital design. As humanistic designers, we are driven not by the novelty of the technology, but the unexplored possibilities for making meaning. For me, the most enticing possibilities lie in the structures we can create for more complex storytelling. Television is a particularly rich source of narrative design problems. Digital transmission has opened up the possibility of long-form storytelling, since audiences can view whole seasons after their original broadcast date, and they can follow story over multiple seasons. This is leading to greater consistency and ambition in storytelling, but it is also confusing to audiences, which opens up productive opportunities for interaction design.

Why create aids for watching TV shows? Storytelling is one of the oldest human activities, a means of sharing our understanding of the world, creating cultural affiliations and identities, testing our moral judgments, and expanding our capacity for empathy. Structures that help us to tell and to receive more complex stories hold the promise of expanding human potential. Of course, that potential can be used for constructive or destructive purposes. For me, as a child of the enlightenment with a faith in human reason and the democratization of knowledge, and as an educator within the problem-solving atmosphere of an Institute of Technology, I lean to the optimistic view.

Working in a field that has brought such radical change to social practices and revenue streams, I have often been confronted by panicking professionals including print journalists, broadcast news

**Storytelling is one of the oldest human activities, a means of sharing our understanding of the world, creating cultural affiliations and identities, testing our moral judgments, and expanding our capacity for empathy.**

producers, heads of movie studies, publishers, librarians, Shakespeare scholars, and deans of universities, all of whom have good reason to worry about how changes in the inscription and transmission and information will affect their job security and the future of their institutions. My response to this very real anxiety is always the same: Consider the core function of what you are doing and focus on preserving and expanding that, rather than fetishizing the current media formats. This is also the first step in the radically constructive design process that I teach my students in the core course in interaction design. It comes from the humanistic stance of stepping back from the current moment and to look at the situation within the longer view of human culture. The answer to "what will become of us in the digital age if newspapers or books or television networks suddenly disappear?" is to identify the longer history of the activity, to retrace how it took the shape it currently has, and to try to see what value it has independent of particular media objects. A newspaper or TV news show is valuable because professional journalism is valuable with or without the current methods of segmenting and transmitting it. The question is not how do we preserve legacy formats, but how do we expand the journalistic enterprise by harnessing the powerful expressive affordances of the digital medium?

As an educator in a rapidly changing field I have a responsibility to train students with methods that will last them over their career. Humanistic design methods offer the best framework for that approach, in my view, by providing us with a radical perspective that can turn the threat of digital disruption into the opportunity for creative invention and renewal.

The answer to "what will become of us in the digital age if newspapers or books or television networks suddenly disappear?" is to identify the longer history of the activity, to retrace how it took the shape it currently has, and to try to see what value it has independent of particular media objects.

"Yesterday's scientist and engineer was a technician, frequently operating in the technical vacuum of their discipline. The 21st Century scientist and engineer have a 'renaissance' education able to use their technical knowledge to improve the human condition, affect change of policy and practice, and communicate complex problems and solutions. As we develop the next generation of leaders who have a broad and deep understanding of the world around them, 'One Georgia Tech' will describe our education—bringing diverse perspectives together in order to instill a critical set of skills in analysis and application. The inter- and cross-disciplinary nature of the School of Literature, Media, & Communication is an exemplar of the unique perspective on technology and its broader implications on human behavior, ethics, and society."

*Rafael L. Bras,*
*GT Provost & Executive Vice-President*
*for Academic Affairs*

# Nihad Farooq

# On Slavery and Social Networks

In January 2011, despite the Egyptian government's attempt to establish a communications blocade, thousands of young Egyptians blanketed the streets nationwide, demanding an end to Hosni Mubarak's 30-year rule. Journalists and social media theorists have highlighted the significant role played by Facebook, Twitter, and blogs in contributing to the diffuse yet organized nature of these protests; the use of social media enabled an unprecedented number of separate demonstrations to occur simultaneously on what was dubbed beforehand—in online posts and tweets—as an upcoming "day of wrath."

The Arab Spring, however, is not the first revolution driven by social networks; in the Americas, especially within the complex structure of New World slavery, the power of social networks to achieve such momentum has a long history and a vast geographical terrain, from Virginia to Trinidad, from Veracruz to Antigua, and beyond. We can look back, for example, to the German Coast Uprising of January 1811, in which slaves spread word of a planned revolt among hundreds of their peers at plantations up and down the east coast of the Mississippi. Although Charles Deslondes is often credited as the hero of the uprising, historians have now pointed to as many as 11 separate leaders, representing various ethnic groups, and a vast network of communication that extended back through the Caribbean.

In my research and teaching here at Georgia Tech, I encourage my students to think about how we can use our contemporary understandings of technology and its various functions to better understand the political and cultural work of literature across a broad span of history. How might we use our postmodern understandings of virtual worlds, disembodied selves, and global connectivity to help us visualize and imagine the perpetual movement of cultures across time and space, through the diffuse circulation and exchange of languages, experiences, epistemologies, and traditions?

My own research on slavery and social networks, for example, examines the ways in which earlier acts of social and political resistance thwarted narratives of origin and traceability in the same way that some of today's resistance networks do, even as they rely on hierarchical structures and institutions to (sometimes surreptitiously) achieve their aims. By linking contemporary network theory to historical and contemporary acts of political resistance and community formation, I employ a humanistic lens that is necessarily technological. I ask students to consider how virtual networks, like those that have inspired or tracked contempo-

rary democratization movements in Tunisia, Cairo, and Iran (a.k.a., the "Twitter Revolution") transform the logic of destabilization and chaos that guides network theory, into a seamless structure of movement and action. How might a reexamination of slave resistance and slave narratives through this critical-technological lens, for example, further our understanding of the evolution of social networks and political mobilization across different geographies and historical periods? What might we learn from the kinship ties forged in these early American spaces and the narratives of flight and survival they inspired? How does the contemporary virtual community borrow from this unique history of constructed kinship, and how might such a link help us reconsider nationalism, democracy, and family in the twenty-first century?

Slave rebels of 1811, then, have much to teach us about the kinds of social networks that enabled and inspired the protests of 2011. Hemmed in by a social structure that has been historically focused on the problems of alienation, discontinuity, and the dissolution of 'natural' categories of kinship, slave communities (whose formation and persistence—in the face of great odds—is in itself an act of rebellion) might actually offer contemporary readers new insight into the convergence, the function, and the power of diffuse social and political networks throughout history. For as slave ships made the same journeys and marked the same patterns of travel across and back through Atlantic ports, as family and community members heard information—even misinformation—about their kin adrift in the New World, and as new patterns of kinship were formed, based on common struggle and common cause, a new kind of network collectivity emerged. This new collectivity was not tied to the traditional organizations of geography nor biology nor national affiliation, but, like today's global internet, was a collectivity that emerged and strengthened precisely because of its lack of boundaries, traceable origin, or kin—anonymity and alienation became acts of strategic camouflage: Because they were suddenly nowhere and no one, they could use information to be anyone anywhere—a collective action united against oppression.

**The Arab Spring, however, is not the first revolution driven by social networks; in the Americas, especially within the complex structure of New World slavery, the power of social networks to achieve such momentum has a long history and a vast geographical terrain [...]**

By locating my study of eighteenth- and nineteenth-century slave networks within a contemporary discourse of social network theory (particularly recent scholarship that discusses the global internet as a space of queer or creolized networks),

I am able to help students think outside traditional paradigms of community, national, and familial organization. Just as contemporary social media prioritizes overlapping functions and strategic alliances above traditional kinship ties, so many slave networks generally functioned and were organized—by necessity—outside traditional paradigms of family, home, and national allegiance. The diverse community of strangers in the New World who organized plots and created a vast network of information mirrors the organizational structure of the global internet. But while we often pathologize these kinds of networks in our contemporary era (i.e., terrorist cells, disease outbreaks), a backward glance at slave networks reveals the politically progressive implications of loose ties and networked mobilities for inciting democratic social movements, such as the abolition of slavery and the collapse of dictatorial regimes.

My research and pedagogical investments are thus inherently interdisciplinary and rooted in the technological, as I work from the premise that race—as a diasporic, performative, and infinitely mobile act—is itself a technology, and one that is central, not peripheral, to understanding how communities and nations are made and unmade. The emergence, survival, and the spread of community networks are forged by these mobile and mobilizing racial alliances, and backed, of course, by a shared desire for freedom that was strategically, if not ideologically, parallel to the founding propositions of New World settlement.

My research and pedagogical investments are thus inherently interdisciplinary and rooted in the technological, as I work from the premise that race—as a diasporic, performative, and infinitely mobile act—is itself a technology, and one that is central, not peripheral, to understanding how communities and nations are made and unmade.

# Krystina Madej

# History of Narrative as Material Practice: Interpreting Communication Technologies

**Frame of Reference:**

*History* lets us put a subject in a broader context, giving it depth, and us perspective. When we know how communication media have been used in the past, we gain both objectivity about the way they are used today and an intimation of how they may be put to use in the future. Without knowledge of history, our world is both small and beyond our understanding.

*Narrative* is implicit in the practice of communication. Whether orally, visually (text, image), or digitally (static, moving, interactive), we share and exchange information through stories. Without stories we cannot link facts, make them our own, and dialogue with others to share our ideas.

*Material practice* refers to the making and use of material culture, or, the artifact. For narrative this takes us from the first images on cave walls 40,000 years ago to today's tweets on mobile phones. Material practice attends to and is concordant with culture; it underlines that material things are not isolated objects; they have agency and they structure behavior.

**Narrative**

In both 2001 and 2003 the Smithsonian Institute hosted conferences on "Storytelling: Passport to the 21st Century" including speakers such as John Seely Brown, Chief Scientist at Xerox, Larry Prusak, Executive Director of the IBM Institute of Knowledge, and Steve Dinning, former director of Knowledge Management at the World Bank. The conference highlighted the use of narrative to achieve practical outcomes. Conference speakers explored storytelling and suggested it would become a key component of "managing communications, education, training, and innovation" in the new century. This conference envisioned a new world order and value for narrative. When Dinning had first explored the possibilities of using narrative in business, however, as he tells us in *The Springboard: How Storytelling Ignites Action in Knowledge-Era Organizations* (2012, p. xv), the reality exposed a different perspective:

*I quickly found I was living in an age when storytelling was suspect. Scientists derided it. Philosophers threatened to censor it. Logicians had difficulty in depicting it. Management theorists generally ignored it. And storytelling's bad press was not new. It had been disreputable for several millennia, ever since Plato identified poets and storytellers as dangerous fellows who put unreliable knowledge in the heads of children and hence would be subject to strict censorship in The Republic.*

## Why Such Suspicion?

Our society espouses the scientific method as the best way of knowing. The rationalism (logic) of the Greeks and the empiricism (direct observation, recording and monitoring of the world) of the seventeenth and eighteenth century are two identifiable and dominant aspects of the scientific tradition. This rational-empirical approach came to characterize scientific inquiry and was adopted for the study of society in the nineteenth century by the French philosopher August Comte. Comte believed society could be studied scientifically and understood objectively through observation in a logical and rational manner rather than through religion and metaphysics. He called this scientific approach "positivism." The positivist view has been challenged over the centuries by "relativists" who argue that there is no final truth about which we can all agree. Theories of how we know have changed over the years to include the value of perception, dialectics, and mysticism, among others. Yet the belief that there is an objective world which can be known, and known objectively (objectivism), and the authority of the scientific method, still characterize our own time and many of our research communities.

## Narrative Turn

During the first half of the nineteenth century a "Linguistic Turn" occurred in the fields of philosophy, the humanities, and the social sciences that had its beginning in the theories of the Swiss linguist Ferdinand de Saussure. Saussure centered his research on the underlying system of language, in the vein of scientific analysis, rather than the use of language. The structuralist movement looked to explore the relationships between elements (such as linguistic signs) and in doing so uncovered basic social-psychological tasks/events that are part of peoples' lives everywhere. When they deconstructed meaning in narrative and codified ideas they took narrative out of its normal context and showed that as a semiotic phenomenon it can transcend disciplines and media.

Critics of the early structuralist movement, such as Gerard Genette, saw its scientific approach as pretension and felt the movement was being degraded to mindless technicalness. They argued against objectivity and for the influence of cultural context. Meaning, then, in narrative became inseparable from the context of human action with stories linking actions and events into a whole and providing for their significance. Narrative has slowly become recognized as a cognitive style and discourse genre that people can use to understand their lives and has been espoused by fields of study as diverse as education, family therapy, health sciences, and business.

History, however, shows us that the use of narrative in these fields, as well as in the hard sciences, has been common since writing began. With each new generation, and adapting every media that has been developed to its purpose, narrative has been used to present, explain, and instruct on thoughts, ideas and theories, whether those of Sophocles, Shakespeare, or P.D. James, or Euclid, Alberti, or Einstein. In adopting media as a material culture, narrative gains cultural agency and excerpts the additional power of contemporary relevance to achieve its end.

**Material Culture**

Humans construct their knowledge of the world as schemata, as short bits of story that, with time, build towards a narrative intelligence, a perspective from which they view the world. Since the days of drawing on cave walls humans have used not only their voice and their gestures to share their narratives, but have put to use the materials within their grasp to give their stories material presence. While to us the historic objects we find and examine may seemed fixed, when they were created they were only in the process of becoming, part of a continuously evolving effort to express, with each subsequent generation actualizing a new material culture through which its stories represented their thoughts and deeds. In our presentation of narratives in digital media, we continue that process of becoming far more rapidly than in the past: each creation is quickly overwhelmed by new manifestations as we move forward eagerly and respond with alacrity to the changes in our media.

How then do we interpret the material culture of narrative? Can we look at the artifact left behind objectively, comparing it to contemporary ways of telling stories? Will it fall short in some way, and be shown up as backward?

Hardly.

When introduced to the history of narrative as material culture, *students learn for themselves* that humans have the uncanny ability to make the best of what they have at hand to share their stories: not just to respond to a medium but to use it innovatively and cause its continuous evolution. There is a give and take that goes on, a creation of more than "a story in the ether," the creation also of a material object that is grounded in the culture around it and which reflects that culture intimately. Content, form and function, and media affordability, as each era has configured this triumvirate, are the material culture of narrative used to collect, preserve, and communicate our constructs of the world.

**Since the days of drawing on cave walls humans have used not only their voice and their gestures to share their narratives, but have put to use the materials within their grasp to give their stories material presence.**

**Ian Bogost**

Author, *Persuasive Games*

**Ian Bogost**

# Understanding the "Experience" of Objects

To understand the nature of the universe, let's accept two new principles: first, everything whatsoever is alien to everything else. And second, the experience of a thing can never be verified or validated, but only speculated, even if through deduction. In addition to science and philosophy, we need poetry too.

We usually understand "alien" either in a political or a cosmological sense: a terrestrial alien is a foreigner from another country, and an extraterrestrial alien is a foreigner from another planet. Even when used to refer generally to otherness, we assume that aliens would be legible to humans. Whether from another nation or another galaxy, the other is someone we can recognize as enough like ourselves to be identifiable.

But why should we be so self-centered as to think that aliens are those beings like us? As Nicholas Rescher has observed, a true alien might not even have an intelligence akin to our intelligence. Rather than wondering if alien beings exist in the cosmos, let's assume that they are all around us, everywhere, at all scales: dogs and penguins and magnolia trees; cornbread and polyester and Orlando. Then we can ask a different question: what do objects experience? What is it like to be a thing?

I came to this question by accident. Several years ago, I learned how to program the 1977 Atari Video Computer System, the console that made home videogame play popular. I was working on a book about the influence of the Atari's hardware design on creative practices in those early days of the videogame.

To produce television graphics and sound on the cheap, Atari designed a custom chip called the Television Interface Adapter (TIA). The TIA made bizarre demands on game makers: instead of preparing a whole television picture all at once, the programmer had to alter data the TIA transmitted in tandem with the scanline-by-scanline movement of the television's electron beam. Programming the Atari feels more like plowing a field than like painting a picture.

You can see the effects of the TIA's line-by-line logic in Atari games: the rows of targets in *Air-Sea Battle* or the horizontal bars of horizon in *Barnstorming*. But I felt enchanted by the system's parts as much as

# In addition to science and philosophy, we need poetry too.

its output. The Atari was made by people in order to entertain other people, and in that sense it's just a machine. But a machine and its components are also something more, something alive, almost. I found myself asking, what is it like to be an Atari or a cathode ray tube television?

Such a question may seem far-fetched. But is it really so strange to ponder the experience of objects, even while knowing that those objects don't really have experiences like our own? To be fascinated with the things, from peach pies to microprocessors, and to embrace such fascination as philosophers as much as engineers? To do so, we must culture a new alliance between science and philosophy grounded in speculation.

From a common origin in Enlightenment rationalism, human culture spread in two different directions. On the one hand, science broke down the biological, physical, and cosmological world into smaller and smaller bits in order to understand it. On the other hand, philosophy concluded that reason could not explain the objects of experience but only describe experience itself. One extreme led to scientism, the belief that we can know the world completely by taking it apart, the other to relativism, the belief that we can never escape the mind, and that the world conforms to thought, language, and culture.

Despite this split, for the last four centuries science and philosophy have ultimately agreed on one fundamental principle: humanity is the ruler of being.

Science embraces the Copernican decentering of human beings, but it also assumes that the world exists for the benefit of humankind. Animals and

# For its part, the humanities have revealed the diversity of human experience, but only by straining all of reality through the sieve of culture.

plants too, perhaps, but certainly not toasters or Television Interface Adapters.

For its part, the humanities have revealed the diversity of human experience, but only by straining all of reality through the sieve of culture. Religion, politics, science, and engineering become expressions of human will or ideology, and reality becomes a myth. In its place, semiotics and society were crowned the rulers of existence.

The philosopher Graham Harman has given the names "undermining" and "overmining" to these two positions. Underminers focus on firmament, be they quarks, DNA, or mathematics. Things like sheep and battleships become tricks that deceive minds too naive to understand their depths. Overminers take objects as less real than the processes and circumstances that produce them. There are overmining and undermining sciences and philosophies alike, but generally speaking the sciences have a tendency to undermine while the humanities have a tendency to overmine.

Instead, what if we took all things as equal—not in value, but equal in existence? If ontology is the branch of philosophy that deals with the nature of being, then we need a flat ontology, an account of existence that takes nothing to be more or less extant than anything else.

Why hold such a position? The philosopher Thomas Nagel famously pondered what it is like to be a bat, concluding that the creature's experience could not be reduced to a scientific description of its method of echolocation. Science believes it can answer any questions through observation and verification. But despite our obsession with scientific answers, the experience of alien objects cannot be explained through experimentation.

The same is true of everything—not just bats, but also Atari Video Computer Systems. It is not enough to ponder the role things play in human enterprise, nor to limit empathy to living creatures such as dogs and forests. Once everything is on the ontological table, human choices become more complex. Grand challenges like health, energy, climate, education, and poverty can no longer be addressed as problems for humans alone. The world is not just ours, nor is it just for us. Existence is for microprocessors or petrol derricks as much as for kittens or bamboo.

A new humility and earnestness might emerge from this metaphysics, one that embraces science and humanism while acknowledging the limits of both. Instead of a world of knowledge or progress, let's instead imagine a world in which everything possesses as rich and fascinating an existence as anything else. Characterizing that existence requires a new breed of philosopher-engineer-poets who would observe the operation of things while recognizing that any description of their experience will always remain metaphorical.

•  •  •  •  •  •  •  •  •

# The Poem Is a Bridge: Poetry@Tech

It began like this. In the late 1990s, Henry and Margaret Bourne decided to endow a chair in poetry at Georgia Tech "to ensure," as Dr. Bourne said, "that Georgia Tech students will always have an opportunity for first-rate instruction in the great poetry of the world." He considered it "especially important that, in the highly specialized and technical areas of engineering, science, and management, students' aptitudes are nurtured and supported as a foundation for lifelong learning." Dr. Bourne was an electrical engineering professor at Georgia Tech for many years, was the provost for a while, and served as an interim president in the late 1960s.

At about the same time, unbeknownst to the Bournes, another man, Bruce McEver, also decided to endow a chair in poetry at Tech. He's a Georgia Tech alum, Navy ROTC, a born and bred Atlantan, CEO of Berkshire Capital, and a poet who has published two full-length collections and a few chapbooks and whose work has been printed in several national literary magazines. His reasons were essentially the same as Henry and Margaret Bourne's: Georgia Tech is a great university, I want to give something back to it, and poetry—both the reading and writing of it—should be part of the curriculum, an option. Two endowed chairs in poetry: this was new to Georgia Tech. (As far as I know, no other university in the US has two endowed chairs in poetry.) The university didn't quite know what to do with them.

I was invited, for one semester only, to inaugurate what came to be called the McEver Visiting Chair in Writing and at the end of that semester was offered the Bourne position. I wrote a mission statement. Here's part of a paragraph: "I see nothing antithetical in a major university known the world over for its engineering/architecture/computational science/management, and other related subjects of study, also making available to its students writing, literature, and the arts in general. The making of art (let's use poetry as an example!) is a task that requires a kind of engineering, a kind of architecture, and very real and complex technical skills. Good poems, historically, are made; they don't flow down the arm of the dreamy poet to the page. Good poems are the result of planning, rigor, attention, intuition, trial and error, discipline, and the luck that sometimes comes when all of the above are applied. A flawless architectural design, an elegant chemical equation, a good poem is supposed to seem simple, spontaneous, fluid. To achieve his or her goals, that precision, that truth, the engineer, the chemist, the architect, the poet usually must work diligently, must sweat blood."

In other words, good poems are engineered. When representing Georgia Tech at a function on or off campus, I most often compare the making of a poem to the making of a bridge, which falls under the category of civil engineering. A bridge and a poem. They both make important connections, they have all sorts of things going on inside them that make them stand, they allow us to span the deepest chasms, and the best of them are even beautiful.

Most of the above is from an essay about Poetry@Tech, published in Blueprints (The Poetry Foundation/Univ. of Utah Press, 2011).

> ## The making of art (let's use poetry as an example!) is a task that requires a kind of engineering, a kind of architecture, and very real and complex technical skills.

Since Poetry@ Tech started in the fall of 2002, our main purpose has been to honor the spirit of generosity explicit in the Bourne and McEver endowments. We offer five classes for Tech students each year, two taught by myself each semester, and the other by the visiting McEvers (let's call them that). This course, taught by three or four different poet/teachers, is one of the most unique writing/literature classes offered anywhere in the country. I teach poetry reading classes and poetry writing workshops.

We serve Tech students first, but we also offer community outreach classes: six all-day classes each spring taught by myself, and the two indispensi-

bles: Ginger Murchison (former Associate Director) and Travis Denton (current Associate Director), the Visiting McEvers, and, this spring, Katie Chaple and David Bottoms (former poet laureate of Georgia). Katie is teaching a year-long community workshop, and David will teach classes at Tech.

We've given a class in a retirement home; I've been to prisons a few times (but, unlike the students, was allowed to leave after class); and in 2014 we sponsored a workshop at Positive Impact, taught by Teresa Davis who previously was a McEver and is a nationally and internationally known spoken word artist, as well as a highly skilled and experienced teacher. We now sponsor the literary magazine *Terminus*, already established (tenth issue; average life of a literary journal: three issues) and edited by Travis Denton and Katie Chaple. Each issue will contain poems by all the poets coming to read at Tech in any given year as well as poems, stories, essays, and translations from all over the country and world. I use it as one of my textbooks. We're working on bringing in Lisa Yazek of LMC as science fiction editor/curator.

We continue to host one of the largest and best-known reading series, not only in the Southeast, but in the country. So far, we have brought approximately 125 poets to Tech from all over America (and several foreign countries) to read their work. In spring of 2014 we had a special reading by a German poet and an Irish poet. In 2015, we plan to bring a Finnish poet and a Vietnamese poet. A full list of all our readers can be found on Poetry@ Tech's website: www.poetry.gatech.edu. In respect for our origins, and because of a great deal of regional literary talent, about a third of these poets (and many of the McEver Professors), live in, and/or are from, Georgia.

Poetry doesn't need to be defended as part of the curriculum at Georgia Tech. It is part of the curriculum at all great colleges and universities. Georgia Tech is a great University, ergo, it gives its students the opportunity to study poetry and, of course, all forms of literature.

There is another advantage for a student who might take a poetry reading or writing class, if it is taught properly: it's practical. There is no reading or writing that is more concise, lucid, compressed, and sonorous. Learning the fundamentals of poetry can make one a better listener, and more articulate in every way: any kind of writing, speaking, or imagining.

Onward.

• • • • • • • • •

We continue to host one of the largest and best-known reading series, not only in the Southeast, but in the country. So far, we have brought approximately 125 poets to Tech from all over America (and several foreign countries) to read their work.

# Carol Colatrella

# On Narrative

LMC's tag line "humanistic perspectives on a technological world" offers an expansive promise to inspire students and faculty. As a humanist with interdisciplinary degrees (liberal arts and comparative literature), I have tried to live up to this claim by developing courses at Georgia Tech that encourage students to understand connections between the liberal arts and STEM fields and to develop technical expertise in literary and cultural study. My scholarship and teaching focus on social equity issues illustrated in post-Romantic (i.e., Shelley's *Frankenstein* and after) narratives that represent scientific and technological concepts. My syllabi include fictions, films, on-line videos, and advertisements, and our class discussions concentrate on figuring out and responding to the social commentary and cultural values embedded in these narrative texts. My literature and film courses have focused on race as a theme in works by African-American and white women writers; issues of authority, transgression, and adaptation in Herman Melville's fictions; and class conflict in recent British films. Courses in gender studies look at sociological, literary, historical, and medical accounts of femininity and masculinity and consider how gender matters in shaping personal views and public policy. Students develop skills in analyzing narratives and ideologies that they can apply to study and work in a range of academic fields and to their everyday experiences. The approach taken is that of "cultural study of narrative," which focuses attention on written, visual, and non-verbal discourse.

### What is "narrative"?

In the past century there has been an explosion of interest in studying narrative forms and in establishing robust theories of narrative that apply across disciplines, media, and cultures. Porter Abbott (2008) offers a succinct and commonsense definition that privileges plot: "As soon as we follow a subject with a verb, there is a good chance we are engaged in narrative discourse." Gerald Prince (2003) acknowledges the mixed rhetorical modes of narrative in his definition: "Narrative is a discourse representing one or more events. Narration is traditionally distinguished from description and from commentary but usually incorporates them within itself."

French theorist Roland Barthes's essay "Introduction to the Structural Analysis of Narrative" initiated interest in applying techniques used to study literary texts to cultural texts in claiming "The narratives of the world are numberless. . . . Moreover, under this almost infinite diversity of forms, narrative is present in every age, in every place, in every society; it begins with the very history of mankind and there nowhere is nor has been a people without narrative. All classes, all human groups, have their narratives, enjoyment of which is very often shared by men with different, even opposing, cultural backgrounds. Caring nothing for the division between good and bad literature, narrative is international, transhistorical, transcultural: it is simply there, like life itself."

Barthes's description of narrative is the most expansive and exciting in connecting cultural activities to textual accounts of such experiences and doing so across time, space, and other boundaries. To study narrative is to study human existence, to better understand who we are, but it is also a way of characterizing other forms of existence. For example, fictions such as *Gulliver's Travels* and *Black Beauty* provide accounts of animal consciousness. Science fictions offer opportunities to analyze aliens, monsters, and zombies, characters that may or may not be versions of us.

**There are many reasons to study narrative.** We think and remember in stories. We learn about how things work and how to make them by means of following and developing procedures, which are causal narratives. We communicate and establish relationships by sharing stories (jokes, anecdotes, visual narratives, histories). We like to hear, read, view, and act out stories and to write narratives.

**The study of narrative encompasses a number of disciplines and related topics, including**
- Literature: genres, conventions, representations
- Television and cinema: fictional and documentary structures
- Media: analog and digital forms (games and other objects)
- Communication: discourse and audience
- Graphic arts: comics, painting, sculpture, prints
- Psychology/Cognitive Science: how we think and understand, what we remember
- Advertising/Marketing: how to persuade others
- History: narratives of human events and traditions
- Cultural Studies: human values and relations

**Studying narrative and narrative theory enhances a student's capabilities.** Reading and writing about texts increases one's understanding of how narrative discourse has been constructed and adapted over time and of how different socio-political interests prevail in narrative form. Doing so also improves one's understanding of how cultures and organizations work and enables one to be a better thinker, reader, writer, and communicator. Understanding narrative makes one into a more interesting human being.

**Studying narrative makes one powerful.** As film director Brian De Palma argues, "People don't see the world before their eyes until it's put in a narrative mode." Being familiar with narrative structures and strategies increases one's capacity to discern ideologies of power influencing interpretation. Analyzing texts includes considering both author and reader, for, as feminist literary theorist Susan Lanser notes, "Feminist critique of the masculinist bias. . . has . . . taken the view that theory sometimes says more about the reader than about the text."

**The study of narrative can be the foundation for many career paths.** Fields that value understanding narrative include
- Creative writing, technical communication, web and graphic design, journalism, marketing
- Working in television, film, social media, game, Internet, and other companies
- Teaching literature, media, communication,

cultural studies, design

• Pursuing study/practice in law, public health, medicine, business

In short, reading, discussing, and writing about narratives prepares one for work, relationships, and political engagement. Understanding the dynamics of a fictional world, as one does when one reads a novel or sees a film, and teasing out the logical contradictions of an attempt to persuade, as one does when viewing a print or television advertisement or hearing a political speech, are skills that one uses every day.

• • • • • • • • • •

# Understanding the dynamics of a fictional world, as one does when one reads a novel or sees a film, and teasing out the logical contradictions of an attempt to persuade, as one does when viewing a print or television advertisement or hearing a political speech, are skills that one uses every day.

*Anne Pollock (left) as guest on MSNBC's Melissa Harris-Perry Show*

# Anne Pollock

# Biomedicine and Culture

I am an Associate Professor of Science, Technology, and Culture in the School of Literature, Media, and Communication at Georgia Tech. My research and teaching focus on biomedicine and culture, theories of race and gender, and how science and medicine are enrolled in social justice projects. These areas may seem like disparate spheres for some, but for me, they are deeply intertwined. Biomedical research and practice are human projects as much as they are technoscientific ones. That means that biomedicine is inextricable from our social and cultural world—as the world is, and as we would have it be. My research in wide-ranging areas is animated by the question: how do we enroll medical technologies and disease categories in stories we tell about identity and difference, especially with regard to race, gender, and citizenship?

I received my PhD from MIT in Science, Technology and Society. Science, Technology, and Society (STS)—also called Science and Technology Studies—is an interdisciplinary field of study that seeks to understand how science and technology shape society and culture and how society and culture, in turn, shape the development of science and technology. Since I had found being in an environment of scientists and engineers to be very intellectually exciting, I welcomed the opportunity to pursue my interdisciplinary research and teaching at a tech school. Moreover, when considering possible jobs to pursue, I was reluctant to choose just one disciplinary home, as an anthropologist, or a historian, or something else like a medical ethicist of some stripe—and the chance to forgo those reinventions to be situated in a program in Science, Technology and Culture in the School of Literature, Media, and Communication (LMC) sounded fantastic. Now that I approach my seventh year here, it has indeed turned out to be a good place to land.

From my experience at MIT, I was used to hanging out with scientists and engineers. In my larger STS circles, most of my interlocutors are anthropologists, sociologists, and historians. One thing that has been new for me is that here in LMC is that many of my colleagues are trained in literature. Although my own training was more anthropological, sociological and to a lesser degree historical, I have long been centrally interested in narrative. My conversations with my LMC colleagues has helped me to hone this engagement.

In my classes, we read mostly non-fiction narratives, in diverse forms—illness narratives; biographies and memoirs of scientists and physicians; ethnographic and historical accounts of the perspectives of healthcare researchers, providers and patients. We also critically read stories drawn from diverse genres that are not themselves humanistic, such as pharmaceutical advertisements and scientific reports.

In the lab and in the newspapers, topics in biomedicine are frequent subjects of debate. From assisted reproductive technology and stem cells, to pharmaceuticals and imaging technologies, to life support and its termination, biomedical technologies are shaping our lives in unprecedented ways. In my teaching and in my writing for academic and broader audiences, I strive to provide students and interested others with both information and analytical tools to grapple with the intersections of biomedicine and culture in society.

As a teacher, I am committed to challenging students from across the social sciences, humanities, sciences, and engineering to think critically about their social worlds. Medicine is a great topic for that kind of project. For example, much of my research explores pharmaceuticals. Pharmaceuticals are objects that are easily recognized as being simultaneously stuff and symbol, carrying both matter and meaning. Critical examination of them gives us the opportunity to think about the physical and social existence that we shape and are shaped by.

One of the distinctive aspects of my classes is that I strive to have the students explore nuance in often polarized debates. Thus, rather than having a pro and con debate about, say, embryonic stem cell research, we talk in a grounded way about what is at stake, not just for the embryo but also for the women who provide the reproductive material, for people with disabilities, for people in poverty who cannot afford existing medicines much less high tech innovations.

I find the process of preparing courses and the liveliness of the classroom environment to be intellectually stimulating complements to my research. My first book, *Medicating Race: Heart Disease and Durable Preoccupations with Difference*, was published in 2012. In that book, I trace the discourses of heart disease and race from the founding of cardiology to the commercial failure of a drug called BiDil, which in 2005 became the first drug ever approved by the FDA with a racial indication, for heart failure in "self-identified black patients." In my current work, I continue to explore themes of race and medicine in the U.S. and beyond. One ongoing project, "Places of Pharmaceutical Knowledge-Making," involves ethnographic research at a small South African startup pharmaceutical company with an elite international scientific board, which was founded with the mission of drug discovery for HIV, tuberculosis, and malaria. For this project, I travel to Johannesburg to talk with the scientists about their research and why its location matters, and also trace the global networks of the training of these African scientists. My writing on this project explores how the location of the scientific knowledge component of pharmaceuticals—rather than their production, licensing, or distribution—matters for both the scientists involved and for all interested in global health.

The LMC slogan—"diverse humanistic perspectives on a technological world"—is a great description of what I do in the classroom and in my research. I look forward to further developing my research and teaching here, and to seeing how we all grow together.

• • • • • • • • •

One thing that has been new for me is that here in LMC is that many of my colleagues are trained in literature. Although my own training was more anthropological, sociological and to a lesser degree historical, I have long been centrally interested in narrative. My conversations with my LMC colleagues has helped me to hone this engagement.

"LMC is continuously broadening the scope of humanities research and pedagogy. Whether building a digital archive, experimenting with multi-modal means of communication, or exploring the connections among literature, film, science, technology, and culture, LMC faculty and students are helping to shape new directions for Georgia Tech."

Sherri Brown,
Reference & Subject Librarian,
GT Library & Information Center

# Blake Leland

# We're in the Money

Mid-20th century thinkers such as Harold Innis, Marshall McLuhan, Walter J. Ong, and Eric A. Havelock, immersed in a world of relatively new communication technologies (radio/TV/film), sought to understand the effects of these technologies by exploring an earlier, more fundamental shift in the technology or technique of communication—that is, the shift from orality to literacy, from a culture that could know only what it could remember and recite to a culture that could make long-lasting records of what it knew and thus free the human mind to apply itself to something more than recollection and repetition.

Others continued the work they began so that now, in the 21st century, it has become clear that the term "technology" may be applied more widely than it once was. It still names the world of big machines powered by wind, water, steam, oil, or electricity, but more and more it has come to mean technologies of information, representation, communication. One such technology—more ancient than writing, more ubiquitous than the smart phone—is money.

Money, money, money, money: we want it, we need it, we go to college (and justify the money spent) to learn how to make it. But what is it? The dictionary offers this: "…any objects or tokens regarded as a store of value and used as a medium of exchange." So, it would appear that money is a kind of media device for storing and exchanging a species of information we call value. This only opens up other questions: for example, what sort of "objects or tokens" serve, or have served, as money-media; what do we mean by "exchange," and what counts as "value"?

It seemed to me that in trying to come to some understanding of the significance and complexity of the money technology we would find ourselves working in a number of disciplines in addition to history and economics. We might touch on anthropology, sociology, philosophy, literature, psychology, aesthetics, computer science and more. A course along such multi-disciplinary lines would probably be out of place in most traditional academic departments, but because I teach in the School's Science Technology and Culture (STAC) program, I was able offer a class called "A Natural History of Money," confident that a multi-disciplinary exploration of this key human technology would help us to discover something of ourselves—and the Socratic injunction to "know thyself" is, after all, humanism's prime directive.

In the course of a semester we found ourselves thinking along with Marcel Mauss about money as it was manifested in ancient or "primitive" gift-economies, economies in which wealth was accumulated primarily in order to gain prestige and status by giving it away.

We examined a moment in Homer's *Iliad* in which the poet seems to misunderstand the gift-economy that motivates his heroes, a moment in which the relation between aristocratic values and rational, calculating exchange seems ambiguous or confused, and is, perhaps, a trace of an important historical transition between primitive and classical money-cultures, even as it may be also a trace of the transition from orality to literacy.

We visited the mercantile colonies of Greek Ionia, where the pre-Socratic philosopher Heraclitus saw in money a model for a kind of early, quasi-scientific conservation law—"Everything is an exchange for fire and fire for everything, as goods for gold and gold for goods."

We explored something of the history of interest, and of anti-Semitism, and of the relation between merchant and finance capital, by looking at parts of Dante's Inferno and reading Shakespeare's *Merchant of Venice*.

We pondered the relation of use-value and exchange-value by reading Ovid's account in *The Metamorphoses* of King Midas' golden touch, and compared that with Marx's account in *Das Kapital* and Adam Smith's in *The Wealth of Nations*.

We read Freud on money and then Norman O. Brown's psychoanalysis of the money-complex in the development of Protestantism.

We touched on the intricate relations of contemporary art and money by studying the work of J.S.G. Boggs, who produces unique handmade paper notes, buys goods and services with them, then sells the change and the receipt as works of art. Then we designed our own bills.

In a future iteration of this course we might one day study Isaac Newton's career as Master of the Mint, or think about the way monkeys use money in experimental situations, or consider the uses and future of the Bitcoin moneyform.

What is the take-away, the "pay off" of a course such as this? Well, at the very least we realize that, as the lyrics of the big opening number of the Warner Bros. depression-era movie *Gold Diggers* of 1933 tell us, "We're in the money." That is, the money technology, like every other technology, comes out of us and we are, therefore, always in some sense in it. To think about money (even while getting it and spending it) is to think about ourselves, to come to know ourselves. And it is to realize that every technology comes out of us; every technology is an expression of the vast creative capacity of human beings and is therefore an expression of our hopes and fears, our dreams and, sometimes, our nightmares. Technology is not merely something objectively given, something there. It is a kind of self-expression even as it is a tool for shaping and transforming our world and thus it is a matter for our moral and ethical considerations, as much as for our wonder. That, I think, is the point of a humanistic perspective on a technological world.

• • • • • • • • •

To think about money (even while getting it and spending it) is to think about ourselves, to come to know ourselves. And it is to realize that every technology comes out of us; every technology is an expression of the vast creative capacity of human beings and is therefore an expression of our hopes and fears, our dreams and, sometimes, our nightmares.

*Carl DiSalvo designs interactive software to support local Atlanta food initiatives*

# Carl DiSalvo

# Why Study and Do Design in a College of Liberal Arts

Why study and do design in a college of liberal arts? Because design is a liberal art of the twenty-first century. It belongs to be studied and practiced here.

I can't claim to have come up with this idea myself. It's an argument made by Richard Buchanan, a design scholar with a background in philosophy and rhetoric. More specific than just claiming design as a liberal art, for Buchanan, design is a contemporary form of rhetoric. Today, too often rhetoric is dismissed. To call something "rhetorical" is a pejorative statement meant to demean another statement as being empty of substance or effect. But that's simply wrong. Rhetoric is a liberal art that provides a structured way of understanding and acting in the world. Rhetoric is the invention and delivery of arguments. And for Buchanan, design makes arguments: the products of design assert claims about how the world is, could be, or should be.

Take any two products and compare them, for instance, an Android phone and an iPhone. Both of these products provide similar base functionality. But how they do so, and the auxiliary services they enable (or don't enable), significantly structure our interactions with the device and with others, producing very different experiences, making very different arguments. These differences are rarely arbitrary or accidental, they are made through processes of design: in engineering, industrial design, software architecture, interface design, and business strategy.

So, by studying design as a form of rhetoric, we acknowledge the character and agency of the things we make. This seems especially relevant for a college of liberal arts embedded in technology institute. And in addition to studying design as a form of rhetoric, we can also practice design as a form of rhetoric: we can engage in the conception, planning, and making of things as not just a problem solving activity, but as an activity that explicitly strives to shape society by articulating individual and collective desires and values. The field of design is vast. If you ask some design scholars, it encompasses all technical and professional practice. It's too vast for any one person to study. My interests lie in two specific areas of design:

The first is speculative design: a practice of design concerned with futures. Designers who practice speculative design often create fantastical future products or services. It's similar to science fiction (in fact, some people call it design fiction), but instead of basing these explorations in narrative text, it's done through physical and digital prototypes and images. In the best cases, these prototypes and images function to reveal potential implications of future technologies in ways that are both compelling and accessible. But often these prototypes and images require interpretation. That's part of my research—interpreting the speculative design to understand the implicit arguments in these works and how these arguments are communicated through form and interaction.

The second field of design I work in is participatory design: a practice of design concerned with enabling people who aren't trained designers to engage design. Sometimes this is also referred to as co-design—suggestive of a cooperative approach to designing. One scholarly aspect of this work deals with methods: how to structure these engagements and enable creativity, learning, and change in the process, in effect, how to enable others to make arguments through design. Another scholarly aspect of this work deals with the politics of participatory design: how co-operative approaches do or do not model political ideologies. When designers and publics work together, what arguments are being made about democracy in the twenty-first century?

The topics of speculative design and participatory design are present in many of the classes I teach. But they are not the only topics of design I teach. Just as a student has to master writing and speaking before crafting a compelling speech, so too are their foundational aspects of design. These include both material skills, such as visualization, and thinking skills, known as "design thinking". What's important in teaching these skills in that they are not taught as just grammar, not simply rules to be followed. Rather, in the tradition of rhetoric, in the tradition of design as a liberal art, they are skills that comprise the foundation of an approach to making the world that is both informed and impassioned and recognizes the power and responsibility we have as faculty, students, and scholars at a premier technical institute.

# Today, too often rhetoric is dismissed. To call something "rhetorical" is a pejorative statement meant to demean another statement as being empty of substance or effect. But that's simply wrong.

# Melissa Foulger

# The Performing Arts in a Technological World

*"I regard the theatre as the greatest of all art forms, the most immediate way in which a human being can share with another the sense of what it is to be a human being."*

— Thornton Wilder

DramaTech Theatre was founded upon the mission of "encouraging the creative talents of Georgia Tech's future engineers, managers, architects, scientists, and leaders: talents that might otherwise never fully develop in the world of calculators and computers." Through multiple productions ranging from improvisation to Broadway musicals, world premieres to variety shows, DramaTech has spent over 60 years asking students to push the bounds of creativity to create quality performances for the rest of campus. More importantly, it has been asking students to find their humanity and their creativity.

Employers today want more than students who have excelled in their majors. They are looking for people who have other assets such as flexibility, problem solving abilities and interpersonal skills. The arts are an integral part of preparing students for the 21st-century workforce. In *The Arts and the Creation of the Mind* (2002, p. 70—92), Dr. Elliot W. Eisner identified key competencies of cognitive growth that are developed through arts education and enhance skill development in preparation for a career including

- perception of relationships;
- skills in finding multiple solutions to problems;
- attention to nuance;
- adaptability;
- decision-making skills; and
- visualization of goals and outcomes.

The theatre provides an incubator for development of these skills. It requires a group of people to come together as a team to create a performance. They must work together. They must problem solve. They must pay attention to detail; otherwise the show will not go on. And the show must go on—even at Georgia Tech.

When I tell people what I do, the question most often asked of me is "there's theatre at Georgia Tech?" My answer is always a resounding "yes". As the Artistic Director of DramaTech and an instructor of classes that focus on theatrical performance and production, it is my mission to illuminate the necessity for arts in the world of science and technology. The function of my job is to do just what Thornton Wilder says, to afford students the opportunity to "share with [one] another the sense of what it is to be a human being."

So, DramaTech thrives at Tech because it too is a laboratory. In this setting, students are given access to a theatrical space to experiment and create. They learn through a model of peer mentorship and advisement. Don't know how to hang and focus a light? Another can teach you. Never used a sewing machine? An alumnus can teach you. Want to learn how to make walls of stone from Styrofoam? Just ask and we'll bring in a local theatre professional to teach a workshop. Students are starving to learn more about the arts. They take their job seriously and are deeply committed, often matching their academic hours with hours at the theatre.

Even more exciting is the opportunity that these students receive to learn the skills that Eisner says are necessary for the current market. In production, we work in teams. This requires us to communicate about their designs and to problem solve how all of the components can cohesively come together. Students navigate the rocky landscape of leadership in a peer setting—exploring when it is appropriate to be a leader or a friend. The importance of deadlines and planning becomes tantamount as they navigate

the time constraints of the busy Georgia Tech academic life. Finally, we take risks—trying to enhance the theatrical experience with current innovation.

Recently, DramaTech worked on an adaptation of Haruki Murakami's *after the quake* in which a Microsoft Kinect was used to track the gestures of an actor. The goal of the Kinect's output was to aid in the amplification of the emotions during specific storytelling scenes. This piece of technology was developed from a Special Topics class that I co-taught with a Digital Media PhD candidate that focused on technology in performance. Students were introduced to the play and then worked in teams to develop different technologies they thought would work with the production. Through a series of pitch processes, several different technologies were devised and the Kinect was chosen as the final product to be created for the production. Students worked on coding the Kinect and building the hardware in order to give a demonstration by the end of the semester (which they were able to do successfully). We were then able to continue to implement the Kinect gesture tracking system into the final production with great success.

Regularly, students remark on how their work on productions aids the group work that they have to do for class. They find that they are better planners and communicators because they are constantly executing those skills when they work on DramaTech productions. Alumni stay connected to DramaTech because they have a close circle of friends that remain an important part of their lives. They view their time at Tech through the lens of DramaTech. It is the place where they flourish outside of the world of academics. It is their home away from home. So, when people ask me incredulously

about theatre at Georgia Tech, my answer continues to be a resounding yes because, at DramaTech, we're building more than engineers, we're creating well-rounded humans.

• • • • • • • • •

"Poetry makes nothing happen," as one poet said while mourning another—and while this line is often (incorrectly) read as defeatist, Auden goes on to say that poetry is "a way of happening." It won't fix a broken iPad or invent a new polymer, but it might help you live a better, richer life.

# Aaron Santesso

# Value and Literary Study

"It is difficult to get the news from poems," said William Carlos Williams, "yet men die miserably every day for lack of what is found there." Literature isn't the most utilitarian field, but it's a vital one for those interested in educating themselves. Its presence in the curriculum is one of the things that makes a university a university instead of a trade school.

What is the value of studying and teaching literature? For some, it is that it "makes you a better person"—or, to put it in slightly more measured terms, that it increases your capacity for empathy. This was the argument of Matthew Arnold, for one, and it was the conclusion of a recent, widely-cited study published by two social psychologists. For others, the value of literary study is found instead in a slightly more practical ability called "critical thinking," which we improve when we learn how to read well.

I confess that for myself, the "value" of studying and teaching literature is something much more ephemeral: I've known enough literature-addicts who were also horrible people to be skeptical of the first claim, and I've been in academia long enough to know that everyone, in every field, thinks that they're teaching "critical thinking" (even if no-one really knows what it is). But I do think that literature represents an extremely important and powerful body of knowledge and cultural practice, and that it influences a wide range of activities and institutions. And more than that: it gives some insight into the human condition itself. "Poetry makes nothing happen," as one poet said while mourning another—and while this line is often (incorrectly) read as defeatist, Auden goes on to say that poetry is "a way of happening."  It won't fix a broken iPad or invent a new polymer, but it might help you live a better, richer life.

How so? For starters, studying literature can provide perspective. Literature allows us to view issues through various prisms—historical, psychological, etc.—that we would otherwise not have access to. The personal intellectual, philosophical and even spiritual ramifications of this should be clear enough. Less evident, perhaps, is that this broadening effect can have practical social implications. Our own motto here at LMC suggests that we provide "humanistic perspectives on a technological world." This doesn't just mean slavishly celebrating technology: it means enriching it, or pointing out its shortcomings, or identifying areas where "humanistic" approaches make more sense than "technological" ones.

One of these areas, I suggest, is surveillance. My most recent book, *The Watchman in Pieces*, co-authored with Professor David Rosen (Trinity College), is about the connections between literature and surveillance, and how the two have "grown up" together and influenced each other over the past 500 years or so. Although most of the book approaches surveillance from a philosophical angle, I also spent a good amount of time interviewing people who worked in surveillance fields (FBI profilers, Scotland Yard detectives, casino security, etc.). One thing we learned, and which we tried to convey in the book, is that people have been alternately enthusiastic and worried about new surveillance technologies for centuries, even as people who actually work in the surveillance industry continue to rely on what we might call "humanistic" skills: analytical ability, interpretation, putting things into perspective, etc.

While some people imagine literary studies as a retreat from real-world issues, then, my own experience has been the opposite, and I am dedicated to showing the relevance of literature to pressing social, political, technological and legal issues. Ideas have to come from somewhere; often, they come from literature (as Shakespeare put it, poets "give to airy nothing a local habitation and a name"). An example: privacy was first formally identified as a right which needs legal protection by Samuel Warren and Louis Brandeis in their famous 1890 essay "The Right to Privacy." Professor Rosen and I wrote an article showing how much of the language Warren and Brandeis used to define the value of privacy was taken from poetry (specifically, from Wordsworth). Our own article has now been cited in several law review articles—as well as *The New Yorker*. I cooperate with numerous non-academic institutions and outlets: I've worked with the ACLU and PEN/America on surveillance issues; Professor Rosen and I recently wrote a piece on Tolkien and NSA surveillance for *Slate*.

My research interests are fairly diverse: I've published on everything from zoos—an obsession of mine—to the connections between science fiction and fascism. My original training is in the literature of the "long" eighteenth century (*Robinson Crusoe, Gulliver's Travels, Pride and Prejudice*, etc.), and I teach Enlightenment literature regularly; I also teach courses on classical literature, spy novels, utopian literature, media studies, fantasy literature, and other topics. This comes in handy at a school like Tech, where humanities professors tend to teach across a broad range of subjects. I do teach a class on surveillance and literature, where we practice honing interpretive and analytical skills—the skills intelligence analysts cherish, incidentally. As those social psychologists studying the value of literature put it, good readers just might be better at "Reading the Mind in the Eyes" when they look at people. Of course, very few of my students go on to futures in the intelligence world (as far as I know...), but they do work in fields ranging from law to politics to finance, and I try to provide some lessons that they can draw upon as their careers progress.

Whether I'm researching or teaching, I try to engage with the latest technology, with current trends, with the issues of the day, etc. But I also try to balance all this with something permanent and timeless. Poetry may make nothing happen, but Auden also pointed out that poetry has one great virtue: in an ever-changing, trend-chasing world, it remains stable; it flows through society and connects people; "it survives."

**Jay P. Telotte**

# Film, Media, and SF at GT

Film and Georgia Tech seem a natural pairing. Film is, after all, a technologically-based art form, in both its creation and its audience reception/appreciation. And its evolution into perhaps the dominant contemporary art form—a claim slightly challenged by its near kin, television—is manifest by a series of technological developments that have left their mark in many other areas of our lives—concerns with image reproduction, sound capture and amplification, color processes, screen development, computer-generated imaging—enabling various other entertainment and educational technologies that are today a pervasive part of human experience. The history of film and other visual media simply opens onto many dimensions of our technological experience, as well as of a modern technological education.

The study of film involves more than just understanding the history, theory, and criticism of a highly significant art form. It also requires that we develop some understanding of certain scientific principles and technological processes that can help us to understand the extent to which, even when thoroughly engrossed in the work of art, our enjoyment and even education are technologically-enabled. Of course, donning 3-D glasses at the local multiplex to watch a computer-animated film makes that context at least momentarily obvious to us, but multiple variations on that technological context condition every movie experience, and we need to become more mindful of how other aspects of our lives and cultural experience are also technologically enabled, as we always, in various ways, see through the lenses and on the screens that society provides. Focusing on films—and television—about technology, particularly on science fiction in its various media forms, can facilitate such an awareness.

LMC has offered multiple media courses focused on the world of science and technology, among them, "Film and the Machine Age," "The Science Fiction Film," "Science Fiction Television," "Across the Screens: Adapting Science Fiction," and "Global Science Fiction." These courses allow students to explore a variety of technological depictions and track how cultural attitudes have changed towards the machine, space exploration, urban design, the robot/android/cyborg, the scientist (mad and otherwise), and even research itself. Through them we can observe how in various ways our culture has sought to address issues of both technophobia and technophilia, even to suggest ways of balancing such attitudes.

These courses also reflect the larger popularity of the genre, and allow us to explore why SF has such a prominent place in today's media landscape. I want to suggest three very simple reasons that might help explain that popularity, and in turn, reasons why we should be paying closer attention to, even, as part of our interest in film and television, studying SF's history and characteristics. The first, and perhaps somewhat superficial answer, is because we can do it; funding and technology have both changed, allowing for the genre's proliferation. A second is that we have to do it; science and technology, it seems, keep getting in the way of our lives, popping up in full view and practically forcing us to take notice. And a third is that we simply should do it; it makes sense and helps us make sense—of ourselves, our world, and our futures.

We can do more and better SF for many reasons, not the least of which is the sheer availability of both equipment and outlets. Films (and more broadly video) have become relatively easy to make thanks to the impact of computing power and low-cost, high-quality digital cameras—even cameras available on smartphones and tablets. Various independent film festivals offer a ready audience/outlet for material, as do established venues like the Syfy Channel and a proliferation of cable/satellite channels. And with that increasing number of venues and broadcast slots there comes more potential money available for developing SF films and programs. If you have an idea for a show that might have an audience, and if you know the right people, you can get a hearing; if you're convincing and have skill, you could get seed money or turn to Crowdsourcing; and if that pilot is any good, there is a strong chance for an airing before a national audience, for at least a try-out. But even smaller ambitions—and smaller resources—also stand a chance of reaching fruition and finding an audience in an age of i-phones, laptap-loaded editing tools, and YouTube. "Broadcast yourself," in fact, is

# But in today's world, big-time science is constantly developing big-time and sometimes quite dangerous technology that we cannot help but run into and be surprised by.

the come-on for YouTube, suggesting not only the ability to make films, but the alluring possibility of almost instantly showcasing the self, speaking directly to an audience of millions.

I also suggest that we almost have to do more SF and learn more about it. That perhaps strange assertion comes from the recognition that we live in a highly technologized society, in a world where we cannot get away from technology, as well as the science that creates it and the reason that conceives it. In fact, that triadic relationship—of reason, science, and technology—is one that we live with, that informs all that we do today, and that finds its way into so many of our films and programs. So we have to recognize how the elements of science and technology invariably show up more and more, working their way into our narratives just as they are worked, almost imperceptibly, into our lives. And of course we need only note how often science is becoming woven even into many popular films and programs that make no pretense to being SF, including television shows like *Modern Marvels*, *How Do They Do It*, and *Rocket City Rednecks*. But in today's world, big-time science is constantly developing big-time and sometimes quite dangerous technology that we cannot help but run into and be surprised by. What our media renditions of those run-ins help to do is prepare us for such encounters, make them somewhat less surprising or discomfiting, clearly a part of our world.

So I would suggest that this inevitable encounter is a good thing and gives reason to my even stranger-sounding third suggestion that we should be viewing and studying more SF. That "should" has almost a moralizing ring to it, as if implying that SF were somehow good for us. But it may well be. If we accept some of the previous premise, that we are going to keep tripping over science and technology anyway, then it follows that trying to understand it for our individual mental health and for our larger cultural health is important. Genre stories serve as important cultural highlights and problem solving devices. Through their central concerns those stories echo our cultural anxieties, and through their conventions help us make sense of those things. The more popular media genres in any period have that status, that level of popularity, I would argue, largely because their trappings are best suited for helping us make sense of, better understand, or simply find some way of being reconciled to the culture of the period. And in this technologically and scientifically-driven era, SF film and television, especially as we deal with it at GT, helps in this task.

• • • • • • • • •

"**LMC delivers in-class instruction not only on the skills needed to present in front of a class, but how best to interact with a diversity of cultures and venues (i.e. news media, social media, fans, and other stakeholders).**"

*Phyllis LaBaw,*
*Associate Director of Athletics,*
*GT Student-Athlete Support*
*Services*

## Rebecca E. Burnett

# Connecting Research and Teaching in the Rhetoric of Risk

Even though I'm a rhetorician—or perhaps because of it—I am often asked why anyone would want to learn about rhetoric, especially when we read headlines that suggest rhetoric signals language and actions, which are, at best, naïve and ineffectual but more likely deceptive and manipulative:

*Chicago Tribune headline*: "Rhetoric won't solve minimum wage issues" (Jan. 12, 2014)
*Irish Times headline*: "Government's 'windy rhetoric fools nobody'" (Feb. 12, 2014)
*Phys.org headline*: "Cutting through the rhetoric on hunters vs. wildlife" (Jan. 22, 2014)

However, an older understanding of rhetoric exists, a definition crafted by Aristotle: "Rhetoric may be defined as the faculty of observing in any given case the available means of persuasion" (*Rhetoric*, bk.1, chpt. 2, http://rhetoric.eserver.org/aristotle/rhet1-2.html). Rhetoric was not only useful in the 4th century BCE for persuading audiences to resolve practical problems. The same principles apply today as we consider ways in which people create, disseminate, interpret, and use written, oral, and visual communication—regardless of context, regardless of creative processes being individual or collaborative, regardless of media, and regardless of modality. Rhetoric helps us more effectively create and disseminate ideas as well as interpret and use those ideas.

**Research.** Rhetoric is at the heart of my research, one aspect of which involves investigating communication about risk. As a rhetorician, I am interested in asking questions about the ways in which meaning and action are influenced by the culture and contexts in which information is created and used, the argument interpreted by the audiences, and the design of information. My investigations have ranged from 17th-, 18th-, and 19th-century visual depictions of smallpox to politics and policies related to condom instructions; from black box warnings on over-the-counter and prescription medications to hazards of social media for girls and women; from Yucca Mountain as a repository for nuclear waste to American National Standards Institute (ANSI) and International Organization for Standardization (ISO) icons signaling workplace hazards. While these projects seem, on the surface, dramatically different, they all reflect my interest in investigating ways people depict risk.

Can the results of risk communication research actually help people become better informed or safer? Yes. For example, my study about safety icons confirmed several points about their design, three of which I summarize here:

- *Scale matters*: An icon needs to be sufficiently large for users to discern what's depicted. Only 76% of study participants (all college-educated, employed, professional adults) correctly identified the body icon (to the right) as signaling an electrical hazard. The scale is too small and the icon too ambiguous for participants to correctly interpret the hazard. However, 100% of participants correctly identified the larger hand icon with a frayed wire as an electrical hazard.

- *Position matters*: Only 30% of participants correctly identified this hand icon as signaling a hot hazard. In this case, two problems contribute to confusion: placement of the hand over the hazard and participants' lack of confidence about what the hazardous material represents.

- *Abstraction matters:* Only 22% of participants correctly identified this icon as signaling a laser hazard. Both oversimplification and abstraction reduced participants' comprehension.

**Teaching.** Like many of my colleagues in the School of Literature, Media, and Communication, I connect my research and my teaching. Rhetoric is at the heart of courses I teach. While the courses I teach have distinct outcomes and assignments, I have broad objectives for my students, regardless of the course. They need to become independent thinkers who can analyze communication problems; understand individual, organizational, and cultural conditions that affect these problems; and analyze as well as create effective written, oral, and visual artifacts. Because the majority of workplace artifacts result from collaboration, my courses include a range of collaborative activities: face-to-face and blog discussions, pair and team composing, peer review, and public exhibitions.

> **While the courses I teach have distinct outcomes and assignments, I have broad objectives for my students, regardless of the course. They need to become independent thinkers [...]**

Students often enter a class about technical communication with misconceptions, believing that it is entirely factual, only uses templates, focuses on skills, and emphasizes mechanics. Are these elements part of technical communication? Yes, but only a part. What's more important? Strategic decisions about rhetorical factors (for example, context, purpose, audience, argument, organization, evidence, visuals, and design, and, yes, language conventions) all influence accessibility, comprehensibility, and usability. Simply put, technical artifacts are not created or used in a vacuum. An unsuccessful technical artifact is one that is ignored. A successful one is always in some way persuasive, convincing audience(s) to read or listen to or view the information and respond in a safe and appropriate way.

To create usable artifacts, students need to understand the why behind the what. In becoming effective communicators, students learn that reading/writing, designing/viewing, and speaking/listening are synergistic. They become sophisticated in balancing verbal and visual information and us-

ing different modalities with various media. They consider socio-cultural factors—for example, ethics, economics, and environment—that shape and shade audience reactions, interpretations, and decisions about use.

So now, jump back to my explanation about safety icons. Imagine students reading the study—and then creating their own ANSI- and ISO-compliant and usable hazard icons that address, among many other things, the challenges of scale, position, and abstraction. Full circle. Research and teaching are parts of a coherent whole.

• • • • • • • • •

*LMC's Chris Le Dantec (right) and collaborator Kari Watkins (left) with Atlanta Mayor Kasim Reed. Le Dantec and Watkins created Cycle Atlanta, an iPhone application that tracks cycling routes and is designed to help the city with future cycling decisions.*

# Christopher Le Dantec

# Designing Community Engagement

Civic engagement is changing: new venues of public participation are arising out of the development and mass-availability of new mobile technologies and social media; new practices of governance and democratic discourse are arising out of the collection and representation of data; new interaction design practices are emerging from working directly in public and community settings. Running through these changes to civic engagement is a new-found fascination with data and with the distributed tools for collecting, representing, and analyzing that data. Systems like PublicStuff and SeeClickFix turn to citizens to contribute data about city infrastructure to help local governments provide services. Apps like StreetBump in Boston, or Cycle Atlanta similarly turn mobile phones into sensors to respectively detect potholes and the routes of cyclists through the city. This fixation on data raises a host of important issues of equity and social justice, where we need to build tools and practices that don't just employ data to support and govern our communities, but where those tools are socially and culturally situated and informed by the values and goals of the communities that are creating—and being created by—myriad forms of data.

My background is decidedly technical: originally trained as an engineer and spending the better part of a decade as an interaction designer, I quickly grew to realize that of the many things that are possible with technology, the only possibilities that truly count are those that resonate with human values. It was at this point that I re-entered academia, first as a Ph.D. student at Georgia Tech (Human-Centered Computing), and now as faculty. My shift from industry to academia was driven by a commitment to creating technologies informed by a careful consideration of human values: the principles, the ethics, and the identities which inform our relations in the world. My position is deeply informed by the humanities through both theoretical perspectives and design practice, and it is uniquely tied to a robust understanding of computing.

In particular, I am concerned with issues of equity and social justice as they are enacted and foreclosed upon in new forms of digital democracy. By way of example, much of my early research was focused on examining the impact of the Internet and mobile phones on the urban homeless: how do the urban homeless use these technologies? How do social service providers use these technologies? How are these uses shaping what it means to be seeking and providing care for some of the most vulnerable members of society? On the one hand, the Internet and data-driven management has helped care providers track their services and establish outcomes-based programs; on the other, these instrumental uses of technology enforce strict categories of care and dehumanize the homeless by treating them as a symptom to be remedied rather than involving them in the co-construction of aid and programs to return stability to their lives. By turning the homeless into data and then relying on that data to inform services, funding, and policy, we miss the opportunity to use the same technologies to support the interpersonal and collaborative relationships between care provider and care receiver.

Another example comes from more recent research I have been doing with the City of Atlanta. In collaboration with faculty in Civil Engineering, I and my students launched a smart phone app so that cyclists in Atlanta could record their rides and share that data with city planners. The City, for its part, is intent on substantially increasing the bike lanes and facilities to make the Atlanta urban core a more bike-friendly place. One of their stated goals when beginning the project to expand cycling infrastructure was to broaden public input and participation in the process of developing those plans. Smartphone apps that enable real-time data collection offered clear benefits for meeting such a goal: it enabled the City to collect data it never would have had otherwise, it enrolled a large public of cyclists in the collection of that data, and it created a new kind of public participation in Atlanta, one that was pro-active in shaping planning decisions. Yet, even with these clearly established goals, a number of difficult challenges arise: the recorded routes make some parts of the city very visible to planners, while other parts—particularly neighborhoods with low socio-economic status—remain under-represented; different kinds of participation with the smartphone app greatly impacts the data collected—riders who record their ride every day versus riders who only record rides once in a while or if they travel a new path; a new form of civic labor is created and deployed and the relationship of participating through the app and through the data collected versus more traditional forms of public participation remains to be examined.

**I am concerned with issues of equity and social justice as they are enacted and foreclosed upon in new forms of digital democracy.**

The imperative here is that in both of the areas of work I'm involved with, the technology enables multiple opportunities to improve people's lives. The open question is which people's lives are improved, and as technology is developed for civic and community goals (rather than industrial and commercial goals) turning the to the humanities is crucial in order to inform first how we conceptualize public participation, how we position the role of design in creating capacities to act and not just products, and how we approach new forms of distributed labor—a la crowdsourcing and social media—to develop collective and collaborative responses to social issues.

# Humanism, Technology, and Performance Studies

**Philip Auslander**

Performance is deeply embedded in human life, whether we look at the performing arts, everyday social interactions, religious ritual, or any of the other myriad forms it takes on. Performance is so intrinsic to human existence it has been suggested that it may be a defining characteristic that distinguishes us from other species, that human beings might be described as homo performans. We certainly can—and do—ask whether non-human animals or machines can perform. Even if we answer such questions in the affirmative, as I am inclined to, we realize that when animals or machines perform, they do so at the behest of human beings—there is always a trainer or a programmer somewhere in the mix—and for a human audience. Horse shows do not attract audiences of horses anymore than robots have thus far expressed an interest in seeing other robots play Hamlet. When we ask whether or not non-human entities can perform what we are really asking is whether animals or machines have the capacity to perform in the same ways and for the same reasons we do. The idea of performance is a human invention, and we are the ones who care enough about it to wonder just what it is, who can be said to do it, and under what circumstances, questions that are at the heart of Performance Studies.

Because performance is so deeply imbricated with human existence and consciousness, it is impossible to extricate the study of performance from humanistic inquiry. Looking at our technological world through the lens of Performance Studies is thus a deeply humanistic endeavor, whether we study the performance of identity via social media, the nature of performance in Massively Multiplayer Online Games, the potential of robots as performers, or any of the other phenomena our technologized environment offers up to the curious. For me, looking at technology from a perspective informed by Performance Studies initiated a hermeneutic circle, for I found myself interrogating the concept of performance I started with by testing its application to technological artifacts and phenomena. For example, considering whether robots could be considered performers led me to think about the function of repetition in performance generally. Repetition is fundamental to performance: a performer who can do something only once is of little value. In my work as a film actor, I am called upon to repeat the same actions and lines many times in succession, usually identically. As humanists, we may prefer to emphasize the art in performance, its interpretive and expressive dimensions. But the fact remains that a great deal of what we ask performers to do involves repetition that borders on the mechanical. Since robots are much better at repeating themselves exactly than we are, they arguably are the better performers, at least in this limited sense.

## Repetition is fundamental to performance: a performer who can do something only once is of little value.

Performance Studies as a field traditionally has taken live performances and other kinds of face-to-face encounters as its default models for what performance is and has shown itself institutionally to be somewhat resistant to thinking about kinds of performance that do not take such forms. Even if we restrict our discussion to the performing arts, however, we quickly realize that audiences consume performances primarily in forms other than face-to-face events: we watch videos or listen to mp3s far more than we go to the theater or even concerts. What I have chosen to call our mediatized culture, in which cultural expression and consumption take place largely through media technologies, is the primary context in which performance takes place today, a context that influences not only the way performance is accessed and perceived by audiences but also the very nature of performing itself. There is a long and ongoing history of kinds of performing that would not have been possible save for the development of specific technologies. Without the microphone, the style of singing known as crooning that emerged in the 1920s and '30s and became a staple of early radio would not have been possible. CGI (Computer Generated Imagery) has made it possible for actors to embody entities phys-

ically very different from themselves with great illusionistic detail. It has also seen the emergence of a new type of performer, the motion-capture specialist who understands how to perform for this technology the way earlier actors had to learn to perform for the microphone, the camera, television, and so on. I am interested in the ways performance engages with and is caught up in our mediatized cultural environment. I look at performers' uses of technology and how media technologies provide contexts within which performances happen.

• • • • • • • • •

## Since robots are much better at repeating themselves exactly than we are, they arguably are the better performers, at least in this limited sense.

# Robert E. Wood

# One Cultural Context

Traditionally, literature, art and science have been studied along independent timelines with minimal cross-referencing. What Western historians now call the Early Modern period is studied as the Renaissance, the Age of Discovery, the Age of Print, and the Scientific Revolution. Yet the events and achievements explored in these categories are highly interconnected. I examine here merely one path through this matrix of interconnectedness.

Even before the print explosion, changes in visual representation, particularly in painting began to affect the way the world was seen. The creation of the illusion of depth within a plane surface through perspective, strongly associated with architecture in the early stages of its development, also prompted changes in visual narrative, allowing a correlation of depth with time. Almost equally important was the representation of light as having a source and direction. Light and shadow contributed to what we would call realistic representation, but also affected the way the world was perceived. The world was subject to a more intense scrutiny both in science and in art.

Leonardo da Vinci is a name virtually synonymous with Renaissance Man. But though his versatile genius found connections everywhere, it is also true that fields of endeavor were less narrowly defined in the period. He serves as an example of the kinds of thinking that were possible in the period rather than as the initiator of a school of thought. Aside from his famous paintings, Leonardo is best known for his studies of flight. But to my mind, his most remarkable characteristic is his tendency to connect everything with everything else. His study of painting is connected with how we see, with the geometry of representation, with what lies beneath the surface. but his curiosity extends beyond the needs of painting to the heart and the foetus. Some aspects of anatomy address his engineering concerns, the comparison of human anatomy to that of a bird for example. Some of his ideas anticipate a heliocentric system and he knew that lenses could be combined to magnify the moon. Comparatively few of Leonardo's ideas were acted upon and few individuals approached his range of interests, but the kinds of connections he was making grew from a way of looking at the world strongly connected with changes in visual representation.

Galileo's scientific work and its dissemination fully reflect the literacies of the era and the increased pace of the communication of ideas. Galileo's famous astronomical discoveries were precipitated by the news that someone was using lenses in Northern Europe to look at the heavens. Lens grinding had been available in

Italy at least since the thirteenth century and the theory for constructing a telescope perhaps since Euclid. Galileo's discoveries of the topography of the moon, a host of previously unknown stars, and four of the moons of Jupiter made such a striking impact on Europe because he was able to promulgate his findings through a printed book, *Siderius Nuncius* (*The Starry Messenger*). Part of the accessibility of his book results from his rhetorical skill, but a further factor is his skill as a draughtsman and the visual literacy of his audience. For he explains the general topography of mountains and craters through the way light strikes a landscape at sunrise. Granted the analogy would have been applicable in any era, but that it seemed the most natural way to explain his observations seems characteristic of a particular way of looking. Later in his career in his *Letters on Sunspots*, Galileo speaks of the perspective representation of a sphere to explain his argument that the horizontal foreshortening of the sunspots as they reached the visible edge of the sun argued that they were on or near the surface of the sun. But the more powerful the book became as an instrument of communication, the more dangerous it became.

Print was the great accelerator. In astronomy, the work of Copernicus was published after his death leaving him clear of controversy, but with an accessible legacy in print. A minority view could be successfully circulated in print. Later astronomers Kepler and Galileo had access to each other's published work. Because their research projects were independent, they were able to proceed to results using different assumptions. Kepler was inclined to privilege Platonic solids; Galileo insisted that no form in nature had other than a utilitarian value. Publishing also made possible an appeal to a wider public and an argument for a new methodology and a new world view. Print enabled political pamphlets, the distribution of vernacular translations of the *Bible*, and the print battles of Reformation and Counter-Reformation.

One can hardly distinguish the religious struggles of the period from the political struggles and the power of the book provoked the exercise of power over the book. The vernacular languages of the various regions of Europe were becoming suitable for cultural and scientific work. The translation of the *Bible*, Christianity's most important book, into various vernaculars was one of the primary endeavors of the Protestant Reformation. For Roman Catholicism, the imprimatur (literally, let it be printed) was an attempt to control the promulgation of subversive ideas. In this context, the struggle between Galileo and the Inquisition, often seen as a battle between Science and Religion takes on further dimensions. The topic of Galileo's book, *The Dialogue of the Two World Systems*, challenged no doc-

> **Publishing also made possible an appeal to a wider public and an argument for a new methodology and a new world view.**

trine. It is perhaps Galileo's least scientific book, containing a number of traditional arguments, no new evidence, and even a misconception about the tides. But books have an unusual property. What is suppressed is deemed important and becomes more powerful than before. One might view the conflict more as a struggle against a technology than against a scientific theory.

As I have suggested, this is a single thread of associations that begins to explore the rich interactions that constitute the fabric of human endeavor. We can never fully understand any aspect of human culture—the scientific, the technological, or the artistic—in isolation.

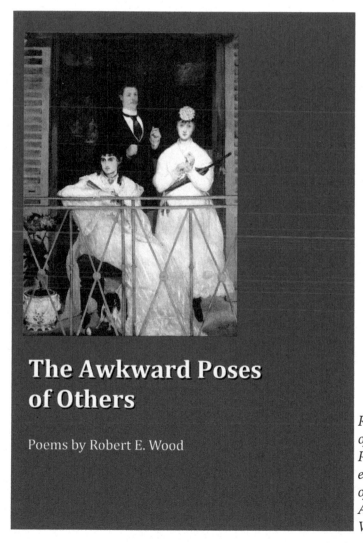

**The Awkward Poses of Others**

Poems by Robert E. Wood

*Robert E. Wood's book of poetry, The Awkward Poses of Others, which earned him the Author of the Year in Poetry Award by the Georgia Writers Association*

"Georgia Tech scientists and engineers deal in the measurable, the observable, the quantifiable, and the testable. We can tell you what, when, and where, how big, how little, how hot, how cold, how fast, how slow…almost anything that you could express in numbers or other data. But the why, the why not, and the what next—answers to those questions represent the invisible, unpredictable, immeasurable context undergirding the exacting, nitty-gritty work of science. Those perspectives are not science or technology themselves, but they always hover nearby. Our LMC disciplines equip Georgia Tech students to make the connection."

Dr. G. P. "Bud" Peterson
President, Georgia Tech

# TyAnna Herrington

# Technological Empowerment in a Human World

*technology:*
the use of science in industry, engineering, etc., to invent useful things or to solve problems; a manner of accomplishing a task especially using technical processes, methods, or knowledge new technologies for information storage

*humanism:*
a doctrine, attitude, or way of life centered on human interests or values; especially : a philosophy that usually rejects supernaturalism and stresses an individual›s dignity and worth and capacity for self-realization through reason (*Merriam-Webster Dictionary*)

Technology is an implement for humanistic enterprises, noted for its impact even in prehistory. Denise Schmandt-Besserat discovered that clay "tokens," which represented quantities of livestock, foodstuffs, or other commodities, enabled trade and the development of societal interaction. Walter Ong demonstrated that humans progressing from oral to literate cultures used writing technology to advance cultural interactions through travel and commerce and to enable evolutionary human thought processes.

The Framers of the U.S. Constitution were no less cognizant of the impact of technology for building humanistic interests. Influenced by the Enlightenment's focus on independent thought—made possible by the technology of the printing press—they created an intellectual property clause that provides scaffolding for the country's most important humanistic goals: to encourage self-actualization and creative development by ensuring egalitarian access to society's embodiment in information as a means to participate in a democratic process of self-governance (U.S. Const, art. 1, § 8, cl. 8.).

Access to intellectual products has constricted in this century because license holders fear the expansive reach of digital technology that allows exact and complete copy and dissemination of creative products. As a tool for expression and interaction, digitization has expanded our humanistic potential, and creators are able to legally bypass a more constrained system of product production and marketing to engage instead in individual publication. Just as the printing press allowed individuals access to informed means to think independently in the process of breaking from automatic acceptance of authoritarians' prescribed knowledge, digital tools enhance the potential for unrestricted thinking, invention, and influence by enabling individuals to publish in text, video, visual, and mixed media expressions with nearly unlimited geographic and temporal reach.

The same powerful technological tools that can support humanistic effort may also be used to inhibit it, since it is not the tools but the human users who determine technology's function. A user's epistemological grounding drives whether technology may hinder or support the humanistic enterprise. Objective knowledge may be contained and controlled by those who impose its authority, facilitated by technology that provides a database of answers to be replicated; in contrast, humanistic knowledge development requires transactional processes that are supported by technologies that require interaction with others in synthesizing information, pursuing argument, and asserting opinion as a way to influence society and support new aspirations.

Constitutional language begs for interaction that leads to creative expansion based on past knowledge. It contains this functional demand, deriving from transactional epistemology rather than technology, inasmuch as technology is merely a tool to enable epistemic ends. Since the constitutional goal is to advance learning—knowledge, information, and innovation—the provision creates a natural connection to considerations for teaching. The Constitution sets humanistic growth at its core. As one of my intellectual property law students, A. Kallarackal, put it, "I think the Constitution wants us to question." And one of digital technology's greatest attributes is that it enables the practical interactions necessary for the kind of intellectual investigation that the Constitution demands.

Inherent in the Constitution's intellectual property clause is a demand not to hoard knowledge, but to do something with it, to make it accessible, and to build on it. Students gain ability to interact in the world successfully when they use knowledge in

**Students gain ability to interact in the world successfully when they use knowledge in functional processes so they not only know information, but they also know how to question it [...] build from it to create something [...] .**

functional processes so they not only know information, but they also know how to question it, use it, and to build from it to create something that is useful to the greater society. And when they are able to accomplish this step, they are well on their way to their own successful self-actualization, based on well-considered, meaningful, contextually adaptive creation.

I have the privilege of observing my students as they gather information, learn to analyze it, and build something new that reflects analytical considerations derived from their own new insights. They excel when my courses focus on student interests, efforts, and interactions rather than my own—when I provide only a bare necessary base in content, and concentrate instead on helping students succeed in their more independent, transactionally influenced processes of using foundational content to create their own new discoveries. Their use of technology makes these processes possible.

In intellectual property law classes, students have used multi-track remix technology to examine music samples for potential of substantial similarity as a way to discuss the elements of copyright violation or excuse; another produced a 3D printed model of a figurine to demonstrate how a derivative work based on original might be transformative enough to excuse the unlicensed use of another's base model; and another student created digital multimedia art with multiple visual and aural representations of music, photographic imagery, and trademark logos that could be mixed and separated to demonstrate how the potential for copyright fair use, or violation, could rise and fall with higher and lower levels of remix and differing combinations of uses (a

police car with a blaring siren would appear when there was potential for violation).

My students in cross-cultural communication classes analyze global problems by connecting online with other students for discussion. And they survey and interview respondents in other countries to understand differing cultural perspectives for analysis, product development, and usability testing. For 10 years, students in my Global Classroom Project shared classroom space online with Russian students at the European University in St Petersburg and created jointly developed proposals, analyses, and formal reports. Without technology, this form of humanistic interaction would not have been possible.

For our students and for their professors, academic undertakings allow us to engage in humanistic pursuits by reaching for answers, building knowledge, and developing useful responses on the bases of our findings. Technology can help us expand that possibility. Ultimately, though, it is a human choice whether to take advantage of technological tools to support humanistic goals or to defeat them.

• • • • • • • • •

# John Thornton

# Storytelling and the Art of Filmmaking

In the past, independent filmmaking was a highly regarded, secretive, risky, and expensive practice. Thus, very few people would lay claim to the title "filmmaker," and instead were limited to "patron," "audience member," or "viewer." With the advancement of emerging digital technologies the practice of filmmaking is becoming more easily accessible. In fact, filmmaking titans, like Academy Award Winners Roger Deakins and Peter Jackson, have not only shifted from using celluloid film and antiquated technology, but have also championed digital film and its streamlined workflow. The practice of film is now for the people. Anyone with a smartphone, tablet, DSLR, or video camera, and a simple editing program like iMovie can create "instant content" and distribute it on the web via Youtube, Vimeo, Blip, or Tumbler. Likewise, online services like Ustream have revolutionized the distribution model, offering "instant content" creators a "socially-fueled video platform" to build an audience and broadcast content live over the web. But, "with great power comes great responsibility." So, what distinguishes "instant content" from cinema?

Each semester, I begin my classes with several probing questions regarding cinema - What is Cinematic? And, what are the most easily identifiable aspects of motion pictures that determine if it is indeed "cinematic? Is it the lighting? The acting? The "look?" Rarely does anything in a film occur by accident, by chance, or by whim. Instead, the creative visionaries, including the director, the production designer, and the director of photography, collectively decide how the audience should feel throughout the film, and then they develop plans to trigger those emotions. Whereas "instant content creators" often accept the tools and elements that are at their disposal, filmmaking is a deliberate exercise that tests the creator's ability to map every beat, secure every location, plan every shot, interpret every musical cue, and plan every lighting change. It is an intentional process of selecting the appropriate tools for the story, to prompt emotional responses from the audience. Thus, although elements like excellent lighting and performance are common in "cinematic films," they are attributes that work together to achieve the greater goal of revealing the story. They are but instruments in the storyteller's toolbox. The filmmaker's selection of the appropriate instruments to tell the story, then, is ultimately what will determine if a film is "cinematic."

Such method of inquiry is significant, because before my students ever touch a camera, or are introduced to the lighting and grip equipment in the LMC's video lab, they must first demonstrate a clear understanding that the filmmaker's "great power" lies in her ability to tell compelling stories, employing the cinematic tools in her toolkit, much like a storyteller uses inflection, movement, facial expressions, and sound. This understanding of the filmmaker's "power" helps students get beyond the sensation of doing something "cinematic" simply because it "looks cool" or "feels right."

How can students at Georgia Tech learn to maximize cinematic tools?

I believe one of the best ways to learn how to make a movie is through practical application. In my classes, I guide students through all three phases of production, i.e., Pre-production, Production, and Post-production, emphasizing how decisions regarding cameras, lenses, color, light, and location, affect the storytelling of a film. We begin with several ideas before determining which challenge has the most creative potential. Since making a film is a collaborative effort, extensive class time is devoted to understanding the roles and responsibilities on a film crew, and to practicing how to effectively communicate as a crewmember. I also incorporate workshops on topics like Directing Actors and Producing a Short Film, as well as hands-on activities to allow students to gain confidence and familiarity with using Hi-Definition cameras, grip and lighting equipment, and cinematic lenses.

What types of opportunities are available to students interested in film at Tech?

The "Video Production" course explores the creative and logistical challenges of producing and filming an ultra low budget short film. Students can expect to complete a short movie, a commercial, a mini documentary, and/or a music video, while learning basic lighting, editing, field sound recording, and postproduction techniques. Occasionally however, we identify a single project that not only encompasses the course objectives, but also offers a significant challenge for everyone involved. For instance, last semester the students in "Video Production" competed in the Hyundai Lens of Loyalty Short Film Contest. Hyundai reached out to 25 different universities to develop and submit a one page treatment for a film that showcases "the football related traditions that inspires ever student who has walked those hallowed halls of higher learning." Georgia Tech was one of seven schools selected as a finalist, and awarded a $10,000 production grant to create a film. Preproduction for the Hyundai Project expanded two months for a four-day shoot that included two principal actors, three dozen background extras, six exterior locations, and Tech's beloved mascot, BUZZ. It was a student driven, interdisciplinary collaboration that involved LMC, Tech's Living History Program, the Tech Archives, the Athletic Department, the Tech Wreck Club, the School of Music, Institute Communications, and Tech's Legal Counsel. With the $10,000 production grant, the students were able to secure locations, hire talent, and rent equipment. It was indeed a fantastic real-world learning opportunity.

In addition, students in the Advanced Video Production course are given opportunities to work on Client Based Projects (CBPs). The Ivan Allen College is keenly interested in collaborative opportunities that "define and solve problems, illuminate socially and ethically conscious strategies for positive action, and connect knowledge and expertise in the liberal arts." CBPs allow students to utilize the skills they obtained in previous courses to pitch, develop, and produce content for on-campus and off-campus organizations. Some of the previous CBP collaborators have included:

• The George W. Woodruff School of Mechanical Engineering: Students completed a promotional video for the 2012 Inventure Prize at Tech competition.

• The Women's Resource Center: Students created a documentary and promotional trailer for 2013 "Take Back the Night" event.

• The Graduate Student Government: Students produced a documentary, promotional video, and montage for the 2013 Georgia Tech Research & Innovation Conference.

• Roaring Lion Productions and MVMedia: Students came together to work on the Steampunk feature length film "Rite of Passage," which is written by Milton Davis and directed by Balogun Ojetade.

By critically exploring the planning, composition, and execution of a short film, students ultimately gain a better understanding of the artistic roles on a production crew and learn to master the creation of visually compelling and emotionally powerful images in a studio setting.

"The Computational Media (CM) degree is a unique degree at Georgia Tech, bringing together faculty from two very different disciplines to give our students a novel approach to thinking about computing. CM marries a traditional computer science education with a deep education in all aspects of the computer as a medium: the technical, the historical-critical, and the applied."

Blair MacIntyre,
Professor of Interactive Computing,
Adjunct Professor of Literature, Media
and Communication,
and Director of Georgia Tech's Major
in Computational Media

# Narin Hassan

# Cultural Exchanges/ Global Histories: Reading Mobility

When I moved to Atlanta in 2003, I was struck by how the city was being identified as "the capital of the new South," and a place of convergence for people and things. The Hartsfield Jackson International airport had recently been named the busiest airport in the world, and my new neighborhood was located just blocks from the center of the 1996 Olympic ceremonies. Georgia Tech was also in a period of transition and growth, and the School of Literature, Media, and Communication was evolving into a center for literature and science studies, an area that converged with my research and teaching interests. The Digital Media program, in its initial stages of development, was quickly being recognized as a distinctive new graduate program both within Georgia Tech and beyond. In 2003, as in 2014, this School was asking questions about what it meant to be innovative, how to prosper as a humanities department in a technical institution, and how to be a model for liberal arts education. As a new faculty member I found it exciting to be in a place that was willing to be flexible: one that could, in some ways, mirror the English departments I had been trained in, and in others be vastly different and open to change. LMC was the right "home" and a place where I—a nomad much of my life—could actually stick around for a while. As the child of diplomats, I grew up living internationally (eight different countries) for much of my childhood, and had lived in three U.S. cities before moving to Atlanta.

The work I do in LMC reflects that sense of movement and change while analyzing what it means to belong or be in a given place at a given time. Questions surrounding mobility emerge in the research and teaching I do in the fields of Victorian studies, postcolonial studies, gender studies, and medical humanities. The term mobility could imply movement, geography, and spatiality, but could also suggest absence, or place-less-ness—a lack of being rooted. Mobility could reference, among many other things, the vast "mobile technologies" that expand our notions of what it means to be a global citizen, and what it means to be situated in a given location. Mobility may connect to theories of space, to the circulation of textual or visual objects, to moving subjects, and imaginary and lived worlds, or be tied to geographical mapping and in turn to notions of home, of nation, and of travel. It could refer to the body—to physical movement—or to a lack thereof, and to notions of freedom, or of immobility and enclosure. Mobility could also imply a "shift," a social or philosophical turn, or a global sensibility.

My research considers mobility in relation to imperial power, and to gendered identity and the formation of new boundaries and "contact zones." In my book *Diagnosing Empire: Women, Medical Knowledge, and Colonial Mobility* (2011), I trace the writing and work of nineteenth century women travelers in India and the Middle East to examine the relationship of women's travel to colonial medicine. I analyze the various material objects women traveled with—travel kits, journals, photographs, medical instruments and tools, to trace the movement of these objects in a circular way. In this work, examining the travel and movement of both objects and peoples reveals both imperial formations and the relationship of women to medical practices and scientific progress. In much of my research, I trace the circulation of texts and visual images as material objects as well—examining for example, the mass production of sensational and popular fiction in the nineteenth century as well as other forms of writing such as medical guides, domestic manuals, and gardening journals.

My recent work traces the mobility of commodities such as tea and the formation of early mobile technologies such as Wardian cases and glass conservatories, considering the interconnectedness of imperial and scientific progress within the domestic sphere. In the classroom, such research interests give students the opportunity to analyze documents like maps, published letters, and literary texts alongside visual images, architectural illustrations, and films. My teaching includes courses with a literary and historical focus, such as "Victorian Literature and Culture," and genre classes like "Studies in Fiction," and courses that consider the relationship of biomedicine and culture. A number of the classes I teach in the areas of gender and postcolonial studies address questions in the fields of cultural studies, anthropology, and sociology. While many of my courses consider cultural histories, my goal is to connect historical and literary texts to contemporary culture—considering for example, "Neo-Victorian" films, and texts, and cultural movements such as steampunk.

In all my work, mobility is not simply about expanded space or movement, but instead about the historical and cultural exchanges that emerge through interconnectedness—mobility is thus often tied not to absence and spatial distance, but instead to intimacy and new political and cultural relations. Thus, in newer research I trace the figure of the colonial wet nurse as an intimate and mobile figure of the European household, and consider new technologies of infant feeding and milk-sharing in relation to the circulation of bodily fluids and things. But for me, questions of intimacy, of bodies as mobile subjects, and material (and botanical) things as markers of an increasingly moving and mobile age, continue to infuse the practices of my research and teaching, and suggest to me that mobility—in all its shifting forms, can be a point of inquiry for work across disciplines and practices.

. . . . . . . . . .

## Nassim JafariNaimi

# Design,
# Values,
# and Democracy

I grew up in a closed and tense social and political atmosphere where censorship was an inseparable part of everyday experience. Since early childhood, I knew that I should not talk about certain books, music, or lifestyles outside of the close circle of family and friends. This experience made me deeply aware of the problematic nature of values in their ability to turn to dogmatic criteria for judgment.

Later, working as a design professional on multiple design and media initiatives, I observed the inseparability of values from what is said, done, or made. These initiatives were all, broadly speaking, human-centered, seeking to support people in their freely chosen activities. Yet each carried a subtly different vision of what it meant to be human-centered with important implications for design. For example, projects that were set in the disciplinary context of Human-Computer Interaction emphasized efficiency in fulfilling everyday tasks. In contrast, expression, creative exploration, and aesthetics were held paramount in projects that were set in the disciplinary context of Design.

The words of the eminent literary critic, Wayne Booth, were particularly resonant as I embarked on my doctoral research, and they still drive my research and teaching today:

Each work of art or artifice, even the simplest wordless melody, determines to some degree how at least this one moment will be lived. The quality of life in the moment of our "listening" is not what it would have been if we had not listened. We can even say that the proffered work shows us how our moments should be lived. If the maker of the artwork did not believe that simply experiencing it constitutes a superior form of life, why was the work created and presented to us in the first place? (*The Company We Keep: An Ethics of Fiction*, 1988, p. 17)

Set in the background of my personal and professional experience, my research is grounded on the premise that values are inseparable from what we say, do, or make; and driven by a deep awareness that dogmatic attachment to any set of values undermines free inquiry, conversation, and community. However, how might one make sense of and thoughtfully design for the many actions and experiences that digital media could bring about and support? My thesis is that we can draw on the patterns of experience around digital and social media to inquire into values that drive their design; and that our understanding of both products and values is developed through the processes of making, use, and criticism. I am particularly interested in values of participation, democracy, and diversity that are dominant in popular and scholarly discourse around digital media.

In 2013, I established the Design and Social Interaction Studio, a design studio that brings together an interdisciplinary group of faculty and students. In the studio we examine the experiential and participatory dimensions of digital media and their relationship to supporting participatory and democratic forms of social interaction. We design and investigate a variety of products such as locative media; interactive visualizations and mapping; awareness campaigns; social and civic media. These design projects enable us to investigate the plural interpretations of values such as 'participation' and 'democracy' understood as hypotheses that form and inform the design and criticism of digital media.

For example, students and faculty in the studio are engaged in an interdisciplinary research project entitled Sweet Auburn Digital Media Initiative. Among the aims of this project is to establish theoretical and practice-based evidence for how community engagement is initiated, supported, and developed through the mediation of locative participatory media. Set in the Sweet Auburn Historic District in Atlanta, we are designing media experiences to raise awareness about the area's important cultural heritage and invite engagement with issues of local concern and interest. Through these applications we seek to highlight and preserve the important history of the neighborhood as a vital center of community, innovation, and commerce among African Americans and the center of the Civil Rights Movement during the era of segregation. We bring together and share stories of individuals and collectives that highlight the complex and multiple histories of the people and places in the district and connect it to the current preservation and revitalization efforts in the neighborhood. One of the key characteristics of this research is an innovative integration of ethnographic and collaborative methodologies to involve a diversity of individuals and groups in the design process, leading to the design of an inclusive and engaging digital environment for storytelling, civic discourse, and grassroots social change.

I left my country for the US in the early 2000s. Those were the early days of satellite TV and the Internet there, giving access to information and opening up the society in important and promising ways. I was enthusiastic about becoming an active contributor to the design of information technologies. I am still optimistic that we can design human-centered technologies that contribute to the development of inclusive and pluralistic societies. However, my enthusiasm is accompanied with great caution that in the absence of critical and humanistic perspectives, our technologies will enslave us, becoming tools for propaganda and oppression as opposed to democracy and positive social change. This is why I am excited to be a part of the LMC family educating future designers and scholars that bring a humanistic perspective to our increasingly technological world!

# Angela Dalle Vacche

# Film Studies and International Understanding

At the Georgia Institute of Technology, our students receive a rigorous training in the sciences, computer studies and in engineering. As difficult as these disciplines may be, the Institute strives to provide a well-rounded education that goes beyond a narrow specialization. As a faculty member in the Ivan Allen College of Liberal Arts and a specialist in film studies, I am well aware that my students need to engage in various styles of thinking. Scientific thinking tends to be linear and systematic. Since it thrives on measurable entities and quantitative results, the young scientific mind takes images at face value, without scratching below the surface or exploring historical context. An appreciation of non-utilitarian disciplines strikes some students as a waste of time or as an uncertain choice for a safe economic future.

Despite all these blocks in the direction of the liberal arts, Georgia Tech students are deeply interested in film and media, because these areas offer an outlet to their imagination, while they address moral and existential issues which any young generation is likely to appreciate in order to move forward. In our School of Literature, Media, and Communication, however, we have raised the bar of Film Studies especially high. In fact, we do not only offer classes on campus but we also make films and study the history and theory of the cinema in Italy through a four-week summer abroad program. This is a double challenge whose impact goes well beyond the book and the campus into a cultural adventure each student will remember for a life-time.

Generally speaking, in Italian culture and also throughout its cinema, improvisation, spontaneity, aesthetic beauty, historical memory, and flexibility about contingencies are valued. Yet these values do not belong to the engineering mind-set. How to reach a balance between intuition and logic, sensitivity and rigor? Thanks to an agreement with the University of Udine-Gorizia signed by Prof. Kenneth Knoespel and Prof. Leonardo Quaresima, in 2004 I was able to take the first group of Georgia Tech students abroad. Since then, we have had nine great years. Georgia Tech undergraduate students have been making documentary films, taking film classes and travelling all over Europe. Most importantly, by working in small film-making teams, the Georgia Tech students find themselves in the midst of a completely unknown cultural environment, and have to learn to be flexible about planning. They also learn to be ready and seize unexpected opportunities for discovery and interaction.

This more free-wheeling model of film-making, outside the controlled environment of the typical Hollywood studio, is in touch with the amorphous flow of the street. This model also thrives on surprise, and discovery. In class, the students learn that this low-budget, open-air, street-bound approach was at the heart of neorealist Italian cinema. The latter acquired international reputation in 1945 through the films of Roberto Rossellini, Vittorio De Sica, Luchino Visconti, Federico Fellini and Michelangelo Antonioni. What Italian neo-realism did for world cinema was to break away from the highly staged, Tayloristic, industrial and artificial realism of Hollywood cinema. It continues to have a major impact even today.

Thanks to the film studies and film-making Summer Program (IFS) undergraduates learn that the reality of lived experience is not something quantifiable or measurable, but always subjective, mysterious and constantly shifting. Their experience abroad complicates a potentially naïve attachment to myths of objectivity in science, law, journalistic reporting, the possibility of difference between good and bad without ambiguities. Without a doubt, a certain loss of innocence is the result of our abroad program, but the pay-off is an increase in tolerance, depth of understanding, and a stronger ability to cope with unfamiliar circumstances.

A broadening of one's own cultural and historical horizons is obviously at stake in a course of study based on the liberal arts. This is why the humanistic disciplines in our technological world are absolutely necessary. It is only through the liberal arts that students learn to ask questions that are about why. Without the liberal arts, they would focus only on how and how much the way they already do in the context of their technical scientific education.

By asking why? and when? the students relate in first person to history and artistic self-expression, while they also learn that some questions about being human and imperfect never achieve a unique or complete answer. By underlining the deep contrast between subjective perception and external appearances, Italian neorealist cinema sent out the message that human interaction is, unfortunately, regulated by cultural clichés and stereotypes. Precisely to break through the perfect surfaces of moving images built in the Hollywood studio and super-human American ideals of good and evil, beauty and strength, neo-realism stressed a quasi-documentary approach, the use of real locations

**During our summer abroad program in Film Studies, the students learn that the special eye of the filming camera grants the opportunity to see oneself and others from the outside, by piercing through all kinds of unconscious or intentional masks.**

and natural lighting, the casting of non-professional actors, the ambiguity of situations, and values such as universalism, empathy, and humbleness in front of a constantly elusive reality.

During our summer abroad program in Film Studies, the students learn that the special eye of the filming camera grants the opportunity to see oneself and others from the outside, by piercing through all kinds of unconscious or intentional masks. Since external behavior reveals more than it hides, these moments of revelation through the cinema foster the possibility to see things through the point of view of another, mechanical eye. Put another way, the camera-lens is a sort of sixth sense that promotes the flexibility and exchangeability of otherwise rigid points-of-view. At the end of four weeks spent travelling, studying, filming, making friends, whenever we watch the short documentaries made by Georgia Tech undergraduates we can all agree about one thing: they are examples of a newly-found personal and communal fluidity during the exploration of local topics.

In a sense, our students re-enact the philosophy of neorealist film-making which shies away from a detailed script and relies on the help of the local community. I feel that our IFS Program Abroad offers an amazing experience also because our students interact with a population historically marked by ethnic, ideological, linguistic and national conflicts. The craters of WWI bombings punctuate the serene countryside outside Gorizia, while German bunkers are still holding up, on top of little hills on both sides of the old border between Slovenia and Italy. For many of our students who are stepping for the very first time outside of Georgia, this means to "see" and "film" history in first person written on the landscape of another country. Cinema is a technology, but it can also become a form of humanism when it functions as an eye-opener.

● ● ● ● ● ● ● ● ●

# THIS
# SHARED
# DREAM

## KATHLEEN
## ANN
## GOONAN

*"A tough-minded,*
*kind-hearted,*
*fiercely intelligent novel."*
*—Ursula K. Le Guin*

# Kathleen Ann Goonan

# Science Fiction, Writing Fiction, and Understanding the History and Social Impact of Science and Technology

The literature of science fiction, which I have been publishing, writing, and speaking about since 1990, examines the ways in which science and technology have changed or may change our most deeply held ideas of what it means to be human. As our possibilities expand, SF invites readers to think about not only the future, but also the past and the present, in a new light. The literatures of SF mirror our hopes and fears through storytelling, one of our oldest tools. A chameleon that can assume the form of any literature, SF is a vibrant spectrum of perspectives, bridging the "two cultures" of science and the humanities. Extrapolating from the known, it introduces new vectors of imagination to our cultural discourse, inspiring entertainment, inventions, and even careers; many scientists and engineers cite SF as their inspiration. SF manifests not only in narrative fiction, poetry, film, television, digital media, and performance art, but also in commercials, design, and news. It is a way of thinking rigorously, and, often, lyrically, about how nanotechnologies, the neurosciences, materials research, environmental studies, mathematics, architecture—in short, everything that Georgia Tech's rich environment offers—may affect us and our environment in the short as well as the long term. LMC includes science fiction-related classes in which students can rigorously explore these perspectives as well as learn to create new, technologically informed science fictional worlds that have the potential to be commercially viable.

The School of Literature, Media, and Communication, with its wealth of scholars and tech-savvy students, is a vibrant community that erases the illusory divide between science, technology, and the humanities by showing that they are not mutually exclusive aspects of who we are, what we can know, and how we can know it. When our technological environment, whether it be past, present, or future, is observed from this point of view, all literatures, including the narratives of science and the material manifestations of technological thought are understood as being a part of the same creative continuum of human vision and accomplishment. LMC's situation in a great technological university imparts to LMC/STAC students an environment in which they can experience science, technology, and the arts not as "two cultures" but as a single endeavor that manifests in a wealth of languages, all of them human and understandable. This humanizing approach to technology helps students learn that, in our technological society, those in the humanities can and do play vital roles in the international community of creative, visionary artists, engineers and leaders.

LMC's humanistic perspective examines the history of science and technology through the arts. Artists, writers, playwrights, poets, and musicians are often the first, as our bards, to interpret and show how technologies change culture, and how cultures birth technologies. Émile Zola, the Impressionists (with their darker, oft-ignored visions of technological change), Virginia Woolf, T.S. Eliot, Kandinsky and other Modern painters, Fritz Lang, Aldous Huxley, Arthur C. Clarke, and many others come to mind immediately as artists who spoke directly about how technology impacts us. Close scholarly investigation reveals that culture is inextricably intertwined with technology, and that reading Chaucer, Shakespeare, or Herriman (Krazy Kat) from a technologically situated perspective not only imparts depth and richness to that study, but gives students the paradigm-changing understanding that the arts, science, and technology are not separate human endeavors, but are instead the deeply connected continuum of thought and action

> **Artists, writers, playwrights, poets, and musicians are often the first, as our bards, to interpret and show how technologies change culture, and how cultures birth technologies.**

that is our astounding human inheritance, which we are privileged to understand, join, and influence.

I teach Creative Writing (which I prefer to call Writing Narrative Fiction), the Science Fiction Novel and Short Story, and classes about the history of science and technology that examine how a once-radical method of viewing reality—science—emerged, how it came to inform our present culture, and what it means for individuals, society, and our future. I endeavor to expose students to the diverse individuals who fueled discovery, technological advances, and cultural movements, as well as those who interpret or extrapolate fictional futures or the present in science fictional ways. In this way, not only will students better understand the forces that shape the present, but they will also be better able to see themselves as potential innovators and leaders in any environment that they find themselves in, or that they choose to create.

In one such class, I used biography to teach the history of science, technology, and culture. Students read and discussed biographies of Charles Darwin (*Darwin: The Life of a Tormented Evolutionist*, Desmond and Moore), Lise Meitner (*The Dawn of the Nuclear Age*, Rife) Alfred Loomis (*Tuxedo Park*, Conant), Richard Feynman (*Genius*, Gleick), Francis Crick (*What Mad Pursuit,* Crick), and Eric Kandel (*In Search of Memory*). They thereby gained an understanding of how individuals can radically change intellectual paradigms through curiosity, perseverance, and commitment to a particular path. In "From the Earth to the Moon: The Sixties," a Senior Capstone class, students created projects based on their deepened understanding of WWII, the Cold War, the refinement of rocket technology, NASA, the Space Race, the Civil Rights Movement, the Kennedy and King assassinations, Vietnam, Feminism, student mobilization, and so many other aspects of that crowded decade of change that we could only touch fleetingly on some of them.

For admission to the creative writing class, I request that students submit a five-page sample of their narrative fiction in ordered to be considered. I do not evaluate the samples for any quality other than that of assembling a group of people who show enthusiasm for writing stories or novels. The result is a mix of SF, fantasy, literary mainstream, and personal narrative; storytelling takes many forms, and none is privileged over others. The class has included students who had taken master's courses in fiction writing as well as students who are just beginning, yet they all benefit from and contribute equally to the workshop format. The work of the class is twofold: students must write and submit two short stories (or a limited segment of a novel), and must also closely read and critique the work of fellow writers. The latter aspect of the course is probably the most instructive. Because each class consists of oral critiques of every story, learning takes place in class, when writers hear how others view the same work in various ways, and learn why. Eventually, an invisible cohesion, a fellowship, emerges, and some writers continue to workshop after the class ends. I encourage all students to submit their work to journals, contests, and paying markets. Thus far, we have had one honorary mention in an important writing contest and another student who won a large monetary first prize in "The Future—Powered by Fiction" Tomorrow Project.

I sold the first of about fifty published stories in 1990. *Queen City Jazz,* my first novel of seven, was a *New York Times* Notable Book. *Crescent City Rhapsody* and *Light Music* were Nebula Award finalists, and *In War Times,* which combines my father's memoirs with an alternate history that rests on the very real developments of the cavity magnetron and radar and intertwines them with bebop, won the John W. Campbell Award. I have given invitational talks at Rochester State University, the University of South Carolina Center for Nanotechnology, the Library of Congress, Idaho State University, the Global Competitiveness Forum, at international literary festivals such as Kosmopolis in Barcelona and Utopiales in Nantes, for DARPA, and elsewhere. I speak about issues that I explore in my fiction—the implications and impact of nanotech, the future of education, consciousness and memory research, attempts to unravel the basis of the human predilection for war, post-and-trans humanism, the possibilities of genetic engineering, and, frankly, anything that captures my interest so strongly that it leads to the deep research that, eventually, manifests as fiction.

As a professional author, a large part of my excitement at being at Georgia Tech is the opportunity to provide an intellectual and creative environment in which students can experience, through critiquing, revising, and submitting short stories, the broad stages of writing fiction in a critical, yet supportive and practical environment. Whether or not one has the dream of someday publishing fiction—although I doubt that any creative writing student does not have this dream—the process of producing a work of fiction creates ways of thinking that are useful no matter what career one undertakes. Taking imaginative leaps is a part of the scientific and engineering path. Through writing and workshopping stories with a beginning, middle, and end, students learn that they have the authority to make those leaps, to devise their own rules and parameters, and that they can hone their ability to write fiction that others take seriously. Immersion in the art and craft of writing fiction is the perfect realization of "humanistic perspectives on a technological world."

I am delighted to have the opportunity to work with the extraordinary students at one of the country's top technical and engineering universities, both as an expert in the field of science fiction, and as an author.

# Communicating as a Professional

**Rebecca E. Burnett,
Lisa Dusenberry,
Andy Frazee,
Joy Robinson,
and Rebecca Weaver**

What do accountants, architects, astrophysicists, biomedical engineers, computer scientists, economists, mechanical engineers, NGO organizers, and military officers have in common? All create and interpret technical communication—written documents, oral presentations, and visuals. What do the silicon chips, prostheses, wetlands conservation, robotics, food banks, and solar panels have in common? All are subjects of technical communication, a broad field that touches every profession, connecting ideas, people, and actions.

## What should students expect to learn?

Students who take technical, business, and professional communication at Georgia Tech (LMC 3403, 3431, 3432) become more effective communicators as they develop individual and collaborative communication strategies. They learn principles underlying communication as well as practical processes and strategies that work in their Georgia Tech courses, internships, and co-ops. They also learn processes and strategies that will be valuable for them in future professional careers, whether in non-profit organizations, entrepreneurial startups, big business, traditional industry, research facilities, government agencies, or hospitals.

The sidebars in this chapter describe projects typical of those in technical communication. The first sidebar provides an example of a project in which

### Creating Adaptable Communicators

Georgia Tech students enter a marketplace that expects them to not only develop purposeful content but also to effectively design and present it using software tools. To be successful, students must learn how to approach unfamiliar projects and become effective communicators who adapt their knowledge and tools to reach specific audiences.

One project that helps my students build these competencies is a multimodal software demonstration video with accompanying written instructions. To create the demo video, each student learns the major features of a particular software application and selects the most beneficial and provocative ones. Then students script, record, and edit screencasts that discuss the software's usefulness and usability. To complement the video, students create software demonstration videos with accompanying written software instructions. While demonstration videos and instructions are important genres in the workplace, this particular project is equally important for the processes students learn. Whatever the specific assignment, rhetoric, process, and multimodality are central in our technical and business communication courses.

**Rhetoric.** Students learn to use the synergy among rhetorical factors (e.g., context, purpose, audience, argument, organization, evidence, visuals, design, and conventions) in creating written, oral, and visual artifacts for diverse professional audiences and situations. They learn that some technical, business, and professional communication is formulaic; for example, a monthly memo reminding employees about the regular staff meeting may remain virtually the same from month to month, with simply a change in date, meeting room, and list of topics. However, the majority of the course focuses on difficult communication problems. For example, while the final report about a long-term project may include a formulaic title page and table of contents, the heart of the report addresses the challenges and successes of the particular project. A formulaic approach to this more difficult communication task would be inadequate (and unprofessional).

The infographics sidebar in this chapter describes the importance for students to learn not only rhetorical conventions related to language but also rhetorical conventions related to numeric data. Students learn to transform data into visuals that can tell a story meaningful to the audience. The sidebar explains a project in which

students produce formal written instructions for creating something using their software (like detailed maps with GIS data in Adobe Illustrator). Producing screen-casts for a demo video and for written instructions challenges students to strategically select the appropriate language and level of detail for each.

Overall, software demonstration videos help students learn how to approach something unfamiliar, develop complex projects, and hone artifacts for visual and verbal impact. Students gain empathy for their audience members as fellow learners. Taking tech comm helps my students become adaptable communicators who use dynamic writing and design strategies and, as a bonus, have a library of software resources at their fingertips.

**Lisa Dusenberry**, PhD (University of Florida), Marion L. Brittain Postdoctoral Fellow

**Specializations:** Children's literature, digital media, and business/technical communication

### Infographics: Using Visuals to Present Information

Professionals need to know how to use visuals (e.g., bar charts, graphics, images) accurately, appropriately, and ethically to represent and describe data. Once information is collected and constructed into a display, it can be repurposed in later reports, proposals, and presentations. Many students understand how to make a bar chart or line graph, but when and where to use visuals and how they contribute to an argument or "story" is more difficult.

students created infographics and then used the new design strategies to improve visuals in technical reports.

**Processes.** Students in technical, business, and professional communication learn processes that move them beyond their first-year composition courses (e.g., learning to create, plan, draft, design, rehearse, revise, present, and publish) in developing both individual and collaborative projects. They learn much more about project planning and scheduling, often creating Gantt charts and figuring out ways to balance individual contributions to collaborative projects, considering group member's applicable knowledge as well as available time.

Equally important, students learn the processes involved in standard workplace communication practices such as usability testing. For example, in one recent tech comm class, student teams tested a mobile app from the Red Cross, which involved establishing a testing protocol, inviting and scheduling test participants, and engaging in various roles during the testing (e.g., facilitator, note taker, technician, observer, video recorder). Each team then turned its data into a comprehensive usability report and presentation for the client, detailing recommendations for changes.

Students develop confidence in using a research-based approach to workplace communication, including refinement of expectations about communication processes. They often work with actual clients in service-learning projects. For example, the sidebar about engagement with language describes a client-based project in a recent course. Students redesigned the newsletter, website, and social media presence for the Community Ad-

In my tech comm course, one particular assignment helps students better understand and apply visual concepts. This assignment expects students to examine their rhetorical choices in visually representing data; to use reader-centered organization, style, and language in selecting types of visuals and design; and to summarize important information using design techniques such as chunking, scale, and proximity that are generalizable to many communication situations, including reports and presentations.

This final assignment is an infographic. In class, we approach this individual assignment in phases, including a group critique and a remix of an existing infographic using low-tech tools (white boards, markers, scissors) emphasizing that effective presentation of ideas is not dependent on digital technology. The students' final, original infographics are printed for display in the classroom and accompanied by a written text (later incorporated into a report) and a brief oral presentation.

**Joy Robinson**, PhD (Illinois Institute of Technology), Marion L. Brittain Postdoctoral Fellow

**Specializations:** Usability testing, information design, instructional design, and online pedagogy, business/technical communication

### Thoughtful Engagement With Language

For me, the heart of technical communication is a commitment to thoughtful engagement with the power of language. Students in my tech comm classes develop competence in communicating to audiences, meeting deadlines, synthesizing materials and information, and building effective and meaningful communication practices.

vanced Practice Nurses' Clinic, a non-profit medical clinic serving Atlanta's homeless.

**Multimodality.** Whether people are working individually, collaboratively, domestically, or internationally, a WOVEN (**W**ritten, **O**ral, **V**isual, **E**lectronic, and **N**onverbal) approach to technical, business, and professional communication emphasizes workplace realities. Virtually all workplace communication is in some way multimodal and in some way collaborative. In fact, try to imagine preparing an important professional oral presentation without writing (for example, text that goes on notecards, handouts, PowerPoint slides, or flip chart sheets). Try to imagine preparing the same oral presentation without visuals (for example, objects for demonstration or images on slides or handouts). And try to imagine preparing the same oral presentation without considering the nonverbal elements (for example, the way the speaker looks and sounds, the lighting in the room, and the way the chairs and tables are arranged). Similarly, try to imagine preparing the same presentation without any collaboration—that is, without talking with anyone or consulting on print or online materials during the preparation, without asking anyone to review the presentation materials or give feedback about a rehearsal.

What are typical projects in a tech comm class? Students can expect to find a combination of multimodal artifacts—written, oral, and visual. In completing projects during a semester-long course, regardless of the particular section in which they're enrolled, students will create several of the artifacts listed in Figure 1. While these do not represent all possible artifacts in the workplace, they are typical of those professionals may be expected to complete.

Developing these competencies is especially important for my tech comm class focusing on community engagement. A recent client was the Community Advanced Practice Nurses' Clinic, a non-profit medical clinic serving Atlanta's homeless. The clinic needed help redesigning its newsletter, web-site, and social media. The tech comm students wrote and responded to emails, executed a website usability study, conducted evaluations, and wrote about best practices for social media and newsletters, while concurrently investigating larger issues of importance to our project such as the politics of healthcare, uninsured populations, and digital non-profit communication and giving. Students had an actual audience providing feedback to their work, and they had to respond adequately to the client's needs and preferences. Students learned ways in which teamwork, problem solving, feedback, and revision can happen in professional settings.

Students' final semester projects included three elements: presentations to clients, instruction manuals for the clinic, and student portfolios, which included written reflections, correspondence, and drafts of client material. The presentations demonstrated the students' impressive growth in their professional use of written, oral, visual, and non-verbal communication.

**Rebecca Weaver**, PhD (University of Minnesota), Marion L. Brittain Postdoctoral Fellow

**Specializations:** Poetry community discourse analysis, American literature, discourse and writing in universities, history of higher ed, digital humanities, digital pedagogy, multimodal composition, creative writing

| | | |
|---|---|---|
| Correspondence (e.g., letters, memos, email, phone calls, conference calls)<br><br>Instructions, procedures, and troubleshooting guides<br><br>Interviews (e.g., interviewer, interviewee, job, information)<br><br>Job application packets (organizational analysis, cover letter, resumes, responses to conventional interview questions)<br><br>Manuals (e.g., policies, tasks, operations) | Marketing campaigns (e.g., radio spots, brochures, billboards)<br><br>Meeting management (e.g., agendas, minutes, Skype, Hangout)<br><br>Memos of understanding<br><br>Oral presentations (e.g., Pecha kuchas, training demos, teams)<br><br>Posters (e.g., safety, scientific)<br><br>PowerPoints and Prezis<br><br>Press releases<br><br>Project planning (e.g. Gantt charts)<br><br>Proposals (both solicited and unsolicited) | Reports (e.g., analytical, progress, recommendation, trip, usability)<br><br>Social media presence (e.g., blogs, Facebook, LinkedIn, Twitter)<br><br>Visuals (e.g., types, including tables, graphs, maps, diagrams, photos; titles, captions, and in-text references)<br><br>Videos (e.g., training, documentary, surveillance)<br><br>Websites (e.g., marketing, organization)<br><br>White papers |

**Figure 1.** Typical artifacts created by students in technical communication classes

The assignments and projects in tech comm have evolved as workplace communication needs and expectations have changed. Workplace communication virtually always is multimodal and collaborative in its planning, drafting and/or revising. Students learn standards that apply to professional communication. So what does this mean in practical terms? The questions and explanations in Figure 2 are at the heart of the course. Simply put, professional communication is deemed successful if it is accurate, conventional, accessible, comprehensible, and usable.

•*Accuracy matters*—Is everything correct? No exceptions.

•*Conventions matter*—Are written, oral, visual, and nonverbal conventions respected? So, for example, all misspellings and grammar and punctuation errors must be eliminated. Words must be pronounced conventionally. Mislabeled graphs and distorted figure scales must be fixed. Design conventions apply to both print and digital artifacts.

•*Accessibility matters*—Can the audience access the information, technologically as well as physically? The print needs to be large enough for audience to see the information. The sound needs to be audible and crystal clear. The digital links need to work.

•*Comprehensibility matters*—Does the information make sense to the intended audience? The vocabulary and images explaining the concepts must be adapted to the intended audience(s). The argument must be logically presented and well-supported with credible, well-documented evidence.

•*Usability matters*—Is the information usable? Just because a document or website is accurate and attractive doesn't mean it is usable for the intended audience. Can users find the information they need? Is the navigation clear and easy to use?

**Figure 2.** Criteria for successful artifacts in technical communication

"What does it mean to teach literature, media, and communication in a technologically-focused institution? The faculty in LMC use their immense passion and creativity to teach our students how to interact and succeed in our technologically rich world with their own passion and creativity. This results from our students slowing down and thinking carefully about the design process (not just to the design output) using both historical and modern tools, using today's technological advances in order to connect with students from around the globe on issues of product design and usability, experiencing performance as a form of crafting, seeing the current technological world through Gothic eyes, and understanding money as a form of technology."

Donna C. Llewellyn, GT Associate Vice Provost
for Learning Excellence & Director,
Center for the Enhancement
of Teaching and Learning

# Richard Utz

# Past, Present, and Neo

The past is never dead. It's not even past.
*William Faulkner*

Cypher: What happened?
Neo: A black cat went past us, and then another that looked just like it.
Cypher: How much like it? Was it the same cat?
Neo: It might have been. I'm not sure.
*The Matrix* (1999)

At first sight, few cities could have less of a link with the Middle Ages than Atlanta. Founded in 1837 to provide a train terminus to connect the port of Savannah with the Midwest, and about 3,500 miles and 400 years removed from Old Europe, Georgia's capital seems to be quintessentially modern. Nevertheless, an alert first time visitor might notice a whole host of medieval signposts:

At the airport's baggage claim, a colorful screen display invites her to be "swept away to an age of bravery and honor" and partake in "a feast of the eyes and appetite with all the splendor and romance" of medieval Spain at the Atlanta Castle of Medieval Times, a dinner theater chain. A courtesy van, which treats her as if she were a noble lady at a medieval court, takes her to her downtown hotel, the Knights Inn. After a change of clothes, she takes a taxi to the Catholic Cathedral of Christ the King, where she attends her college roommate's wedding, which includes the celebration of the Eucharist, a sacramental ritual originating in the Fourth Lateran Church Council's decision on transubstantiation in 1215. She is especially impressed by the performance of members of the Atlanta Early Music Alliance, who perform wedding songs from before 1800, accompanied by instruments made according to medieval and early modern building instructions. On her way out of the Cathedral, a Knights of Columbus honor guard greets the guests who are then bused to the wedding reception at Rhodes Hall on Peachtree Street. There, our visitor admires the Victorian Romanesque revival architecture and watches as the photographer takes pictures of the newlyweds before a backdrop of stained-glass windows depicting the rise and fall of the Confederacy and a gallery of saintly-looking generals. Her day continues with a guided afternoon visit to the Margaret Mitchell House arranged for some of the non-Atlantan guests by the wedding planner. The guide ends his narrative of Mitchell's biography with informing his audience how she was killed by a speeding car on Peachtree Street in 1949. She was on her way to the cinema to watch *A Canterbury Tale*, a British wartime movie loosely linked with Geoffrey Chaucer's late fourteenth-century *Canterbury Tales*. Inspired by the story of Mitchell's life, our visitor ends her day by renting David O. Selznick's film version of Mitchell's *Gone with the Wind* in her hotel room. She drifts off to sleep shortly after taking in the famous introductory foreword: "There was a land of Cavaliers and Cotton Fields called the Old South. Here in this pretty world, Gallantry took its last bow. Here was the last ever to be seen of Knights and their Ladies Fair, of Master and of Slave. Look for it only in books, for it is no more than a dream remembered, a Civilization gone with the wind...."

When I share this obviously fictional narrative with my students, they quickly catch on and research and identify dozens of other examples of how individuals, groups, corporations, and nations have recreated, reenacted, and reinvented the medieval past to make statements in their own postmedieval art, architecture, entertainment, literature, politics, race, religion, and sports. They soon notice that, while practically all these older forms of "medievalism" employ some kind of technology and scientific practice to represent what we know about the "real" Middle Ages, there now also seems to exist a new and different kind of connecting with medieval culture, one related to the ways in which various new media allow for heretofore unknown representations of space, story, and time.

More often than not, such recent narratives, with which my students tend to be more familiar than I, no longer make any serious attempt at heeding what scholars have established about the "real" Middle Ages. In fact, neomedievalist stories (*A Knight's Tale*; *Arcanum*; *Guild*; *Skyrim*; *Medieval*; *Total War*; *World of Warcraft*) are content with creating pseudo-medieval worlds that playfully obliterate history, authenticity, and historical accuracy and replace history-based narratives with "simulacra" of the

medieval, employing images and narrating stories that are neither an original nor the faithful copy of an original, but entirely "Neo." Does this mean that these new simulational media will fundamentally change how we speak about and relate to the past, without a clear sense of origins and originality, "likeness" and verisimilitude? Will we no longer, as first Renaissance humanists and later Enlightenment thinkers have admonished us, try to become ever more perfect as human beings by studying the original stories, language, and motivations of our predecessors? And will this shift in our relationship to humanity's past contribute to the "posthuman" or "transhuman" kind of world science fiction writers and futurologists have been contemplating?

I am convinced that our students, with their strongly interdisciplinary curricular focus, are particularly well prepared to investigate "medievalist" as well as "neomedievalist" narratives, and Atlanta, Georgia Tech, and particularly LMC provide the perfect intellectual lab spaces to do that. As "critical makers" who write and interpret, build and critique, play and create, they are able to shape the future developments at the intersection of ever so many humanistic, sociological, and technological practices. In their multimodal lives and careers, past, present, and "Neo" will be of equal importance.